FIRST STEPS IN MANAGEMENT

Other titles in the Successful LIS Professional series

Sheila Pantry Dealing with aggression and violence in your workplace
Liz MacLachlan Making project management work for you
Tim Owen Success at the enquiry desk

THE SUCCESSFUL **LIS** PROFESSIONAL	SERIES EDITOR Sheila Pantry

FIRST STEPS IN MANAGEMENT

Beryl Morris

LIBRARY ASSOCIATION PUBLISHING
LONDON

Published by
Library Association Publishing
7 Ridgmount Street
London WC1E 7AE

First published 1996

British Library Cataloguing in Publication Data
A catalogue record for this book is available from the British Library

ISBN 1-85604-183-2

Typeset in 11/14 pt Aldine 721 by Library Association Publishing.
Printed and made in Great Britain by Biddles Ltd, Guildford, Surrey.

Contents

Series Editor's preface

With rapid technological advances and new freedoms, the workplace presents a dynamic and challenging environment. It is just these advances, however, that necessitate a workforce relying on its versatility and adaptability knowing that life-long full-time jobs are a thing of the past. Work is being contracted out, de-structured organizations are emerging and different skills and approaches are required from 'brain-workers' who must solve new and changing problems. All workers must become self-motivated, multi-skilled and constantly learning. Demonstrating the international economic importance of professional development, the European Commission has officially voiced its commitment to a European community committed to lifelong learning.

For the information professional, the key to success in this potentially destabilizing context is to develop the new skills the workplace demands. Above all, the LIS professional must actively prioritize a commitment to continuous professional development. The information industry is growing fast and the LIS profession is experiencing very rapid change. This series has been designed to help you manage change by prioritizing the growth of your own portfolio of professional skills. By reading these books you will have begun the process of seeing yourself as your own best resource and begun the rewarding challenge of staying ahead of the game.

The series is a very practical one, focusing on specific topics relevant to all types of library and information service. Recognizing that your time is precious, these books have been written so that they may be easily read and digested. They include instantly applicable ideas and techniques which you can put to the test in your own workplace, helping you to succeed in your job.

The authors have been selected because of their practical experience and enthusiasm for their chosen topic and we hope you will benefit from their advice and guidance. The points for reflection, checklists and summaries are designed to provide stepping stones for you to assess your understanding of the topic as you read.

In today's world a manager needs to be a complex being. Knowing how to manage people, create effective teams, keep the quality and service delivery on target, and most of all innovate and keep an ever-watchful eye on the quickly changing demands being made by organizations and users – these are all part of the daily routine.

Those starting their managerial careers will find these requirements to be very demanding. Beryl Morris's action-packed book will help you at every step, and also guide you in your continuous professional development to become a successful information manager.

As an information professional who is extremely keen on professional development at any age I recommend this series to you. I am positive you will benefit from your investment!

Sheila Pantry

Introduction

Why yet another book on management? Most books on management are written for people who have been managing for a number of years, or they assume that the reader is managing in the commercial sector where the profit motive is a major focus within the organization. *First steps in management* is different. It is written for managers in information units and libraries by authors who themselves have managed within the information sector.

First steps in management looks at seven different aspects of managing library and information units:

> ➤ management skills and styles
> ➤ managing people
> ➤ managing effective teams
> ➤ managing performance
> ➤ managing quality and service delivery
> ➤ managing ourselves
> ➤ managing the future.

The book provides a practical look at these aspects of management and is designed to give realistic and helpful advice to the reader. Where appropriate, examples of 'good practice' from within the library profession and elsewhere have been incorporated. The book is also intended as a 'first step' to introduce a new subject or area of concern. A list of recommended further reading is included at Appendix 1, to allow readers to follow up the topic if they need more information.

First steps in management is aimed at those who have recently been appointed or promoted to a management position in a library or information unit. It should also be useful to those who have been managing for a number of years and now feel the need for a reminder and update. It is the book I would like to have been given twenty years ago when I was embarking on my career in libraries and I hope you find it interesting and, above all, encouraging.

The challenge of management

The last ten years has seen an increasing pressure on library and information staff to manage more effectively. There are a number of reasons for this, including the changing nature of library and information work itself and the influence of information technology – in all its forms. IT is having a major impact on libraries and information units in both the nature and the delivery of the service. For example, the development of end-user products such as the World Wide Web and CD-ROM is allowing many customers to bypass libraries altogether. A recent advertisement for America Online, the Internet in the USA, suggested that it will save you time, 'As you will no longer need to go to the library'! Similarly, there are an increasing number of leisure and other facilities which are competing for people's time. It has been suggested that the role of the information professional in the future will be to help customers to navigate their way through the Information Superhighway. If this is to be the case, library and information managers will need to be ready (and willing) to take advantage of these changing circumstances. If libraries are to survive and even thrive within this new environment, the way they are managed and the commitment of the staff who work in them, will play a major role in their future.

As a manager of a library or information unit, you have a special challenge – to balance the many and varied needs of your service, your customers, your staff and your bosses, usually within finite resources. This book aims to assist you in achieving that balance and to contribute to your own personal and professional development. Many of the examples and exercises given in the book have been developed as a result of setting up Hudson Rivers, a management and training consultancy, in 1992. Delegates on our courses have raised many interesting and useful questions and we have tried to answer some of these in *First steps in management*. I am extremely grateful to everyone who has contributed to our courses, either as a speaker or participant, for their interesting ideas, questions and input. This book is for you.

Finally, I should also like to acknowledge the work of Keith Bonson. Keith is a partner in Hudson Rivers, following a successful career in national, academic and commercial libraries. He has been responsible for all the illustrations in the book and has ensured that the text makes sense – in more ways than one. Thank you.

Chapter 1
The challenge of management

This chapter looks at:

➤ the changing context for library and information management
➤ what do managers actually do?
➤ management skills and styles: a brief review of theories
➤ organizational structures: recent trends and current thinking
➤ finding a management approach that works for you.

The changing context for library and information management

The 1980s and 1990s have seen unprecedented changes in the context within which libraries and information units operate. Although Dougherty and Dougherty (1993) were writing about academic institutions in the USA, the influences for change which they identify (listed below) will be familiar whichever sector you work in.

➤ **Technology** is, they suggest, 'the root of our troubles and font of opportunities'. It acts as a catalyst for change and has the potential to destabilize traditional services. It also creates a tension in allocating resources and calls for different relationships with library users.
➤ **Leadership**. The authors suggest that there is sometimes a vacuum at institutional or corporate level and that this could lead to a potential conflict with clarifying priorities and allocating resources.
➤ **Library users** were also changing. In the USA, there appears to be increased diversity in the student population, with a tremendous rise in students from ethnic minority backgrounds. The **pattern of funding** has also changed with students making an increased financial contribution and, as a result, expecting more from the institution and its services.

1

For the library manager in academic institutions, the authors suggest that these changes have a number of implications. For example, in recruitment, it is important for libraries to attract and retain the best candidates, to train and develop their staff to respond well to change and to encourage flexible working. This meant an increasing emphasis on encouraging upward communication, as well as fostering innovation and risk.

In terms of service, the changes would mean reshaping reference and enquiry services, improving access to all groups of users, developing and supporting end-user services and looking at innovative approaches to delivering the service.

Other issues which they felt would also need to be addressed included collection development and the need to clarify whether libraries could continue to provide everything on demand – the **Just in case** or **Just in time** debate which has gained momentum in the UK. Funding patterns would need to be reviewed, together with aspects such as copyright; electronic publishing; information skills' teaching and the need for continuing professional education and development.

In other sectors, the influences on libraries and information units also include information technology, the increased pressures on funding, more demanding and discerning customers and the importance of providing consumer **choice** – encouraging people to use the service because they want to, not because they have to.

There have also been major changes in the external and political environment in the UK. In local government, for example, a major focus for change in the mid 1990s is local government reorganization and the creation of new local authorities, many of which are responsible for library services for the first time. At the time of writing, the authorities in Scotland and Wales had just been established together with the first round of shadow authorities in England. Many organizations are also looking to market test their library services, contract out elements of the service or move towards a client/contractor split. Others are working towards defining services more closely through the use of service level agreements, customer charters, service specifications or other approaches.

Against this background, how is the library or information manager of today going to cope? Figure 1.1 is an example of a skills model which aims to illustrate the changing demands on managers in all types of organization.

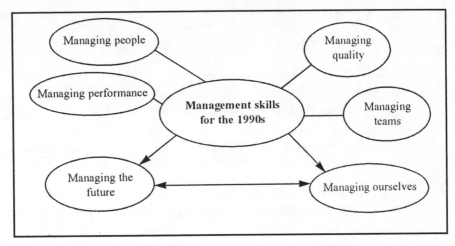

Fig. 1.1 *Six-point skills model*

As a library or information manager in the 1990s, you will need a **repertoire** of skills to help you respond and cope with the changes. The six-point skills model forms the basis for this book and I hope it will help you to feel more confident as you tackle the challenges already apparent and the ones that lie ahead. The key skill area missing from this model is Managing resources which includes financial management, managing facilities and IT. This topic is now so large in its own right, that it will form the subject of at least one other book in this series!

What do managers actually do?

This is the first question asked by most people as they move into management. The response is usually a simple 'The manager achieves results or objectives through other people'. Although this is helpful in illustrating the slightly distant nature of much management work (see Figure 1.2), it does, to some extent, belie the complex nature of the management task.

For example, Mike Woods in his book, *The new manager* (1988) suggests that moving to a manager's job was the most difficult transition that he ever made in his life. 'I liked the clarity of a "real job" and the challenge it presented to me and resented the blurred boundaries I found when I had to direct resources and people towards a goal.' The

3

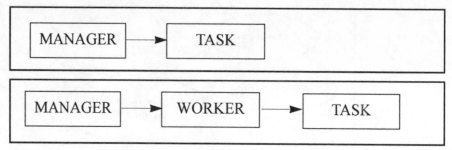

Fig. 1.2 *Simple view of the management task*

role of the manager is sometimes complicated by other factors, such as the management style and approach of their predecessor and the fact that management appears to be a matter of common sense to everyone else – until they try to become managers themselves that is. In some cases, there may also be resentment of your appointment if there had been other, internal applicants for the post and they had been unsuccessful.

As a new manager, it is important to realize that you are no longer judged on your own professional or technical skills, you will be judged on the successful completion of the task(s). This shift in emphasis in the job can be threatening, especially if the person does not feel confident with their own level of skill or if they feel undermined by the organization or their colleagues.

Changing skills of management

Figure 1.3 shows the changing emphasis as managers progress up the hierarchy. At the first-line stage, it is the technical/professional expertise which is predominant, although other skills are important. Later, interpersonal and strategic skills become more critical, as the nature of the job changes.

Management theories and 'trends'

In this book, the emphasis is on practical management skills which will help you feel more confident in tackling your job. However, it is also worth looking briefly at management theories and recent trends, as these will be referred to as the book progresses.

Senior level manager	Strategic			Interpersonal	Tech./ prof.
Middle level manager	Strategic	Interpersonal			Technical/ professional
First line manager	Strategic	Interpersonal	Technical/professional		

Fig. 1.3   *The changing emphasis for managers*

Management theories

Over the years, the theories of management have changed from a hard approach to staff, to being much more people-centred. Frederick Taylor, for example, was one of the earliest management theorists, working in the early twentieth century. He suggested that work should be broken down into small components and workers trained to accomplish this narrow range of duties. Payment was made according to productivity and the manager's role was to maintain order rather than motivate their staff. Taylor's theories, although largely discredited, are still the basis for the way work is organized in many factories, although many manufacturers, especially in the car industry, are now enabling staff to tackle the whole job in the belief that it is more rewarding.

Subsequent management theories, such as those of Frederick Herzberg and Abraham Maslow, emphasized the importance of staff motivation and morale. Both their theories will be considered in Chapter 2.

In the 1960s, there was a move towards organizational theory and the belief that managers needed to work to motivate and encourage their staff. This period is characterized by writers such as Peter Drucker who stressed the importance of setting objectives and clarifying purpose.

Finally, the most recent writers on management tend to emphasize the importance of motivating the individual, although Peters and Waterman's work *In search of excellence* (1982) stressed the need for lead-

5

ership to give staff direction and vision. The key components of their findings are as follows:

- ➤ stay close to the customer and give an excellent service – every time;
- ➤ encourage risk taking and tolerate mistakes;
- ➤ treat employees as adults;
- ➤ emphasize face-to-face management and manage by walking about (MBWA);
- ➤ 'stick to the knitting' – concentrate on the business you know;
- ➤ empower staff, but in the context of clear corporate values;
- ➤ measure quality – They believe that what gets measured gets done.

Moving into the 1990s, there is still an emphasis on the importance of individual motivation and the role of leadership has become even more crucial. Andrew Leigh in his recent book, *20 ways to manage better* (1995), suggests that a manager is competent at the mechanics of achieving results through others, while a leader is also competent, but, in addition, takes a strategic view. In other words, the manager does things right, the leader does the right things! Greater emphasis is now being paid to the importance of encouraging innovation at all levels and, this, linked to recent changes in organizational structures (see below) means that the management task is being performed by a greater number of people and at lower levels than ever before.

Organizational structures

The 1990s is seeing a radical change in the way organizations are structured. This is partly as a result of 'downsizing' or reducing the number of employees, but it also reflects the tendency to move management closer to the customer. In many cases, libraries are now part of much larger departments – converged with computing and media services in Further and Higher Education or merged with Departments of Leisure or Education in local government. In the commercial sector, the library and information unit is increasingly part of a broader corporate information service. At the same time, many organizations have started to experiment with new approaches to managing staff and services. A number of libraries have been subject to market testing and in some cases, aspects of the service have been contracted out. In local government, many library services have split themselves into client and contractor, to prepare for possible legislation and to ensure that the delivery of quality and responsive services is maintained.

Other changes include the use of flatter structures – bringing management closer to the customer, while increasing the amount of responsibility at lower levels – as shown in Figures 1.4 and 1.5. Budgets are being devolved, together with responsibility for buildings and other facilities. There is a constant pressure on resources and an increasing need to justify value for money. Finally, there has been a growing interest in and commitment to quality, including the need to demonstrate that services are responsive to the needs of the customer. This has led to the development of performance measurement and the establishment of targets and standards of service.

In these new flatter structures, library managers are likely to have a larger operation, possibly including arts, entertainment's, room hire or museums. As well as creating more work, as the manager, you may be responsible for staff from a different area of expertise from your own.

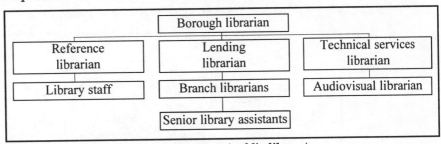

Fig. 1.4   *Traditional library structure (public library)*

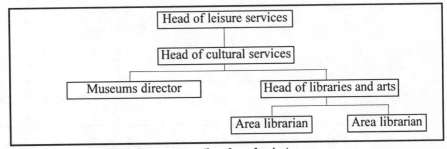

Fig. 1.5   *New (flatter) structure (local authority)*

Finally, to return to the question 'What do managers actually do?' and how can you find a style that suits you, Rosemary Stewart, in *The reality of management* (1993) writes that there is no blueprint for what makes a good manager. She looks at the importance of management choice and suggests that different people will tackle the management task in a variety of different ways.

As you can see from Figure 1.6, according to Rosemary Stewart, this manager's job is tackled in different ways by three different people, each emphasizing a different aspect. This does not mean that any of them are completely right or wrong, just that a variety of approaches might be appropriate in different circumstances.

However, it does mean that certain aspects of the job will be emphasized by certain managers and other aspects ignored altogether. This could lead to gaps in coverage which could be a problem for some organizations. It also suggests that there is not necessarily one right way to manage, that different people will tackle problems in different but equally valid ways.

Finding a management approach that works for you means thinking about what you want to achieve and analysing the most effective way of

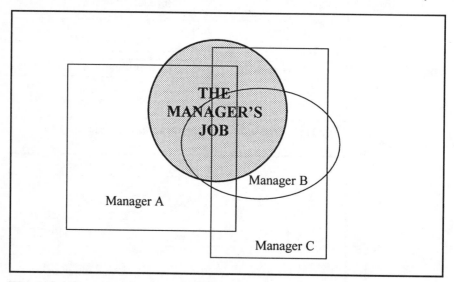

Fig. 1.6 *Rosemary Stewart's management choice*

getting there. You will see in Chapter 2 that different management styles will be appropriate in certain circumstances and with different staff; for example, even if your predecessor has been autocratic, you can and should decide to be different.

Rosemary Stewart's work also reminds us that, as managers, we have to be able to exercise judgment and make decisions based on analysing options and their possible consequences. The 'right' way forward is seldom as obvious as we would like – if it were, management would be very simple and straightforward! Analysing the different options open to us and making a reasoned choice is one of the major characteristics of a good manager.

Summary

This chapter has introduced some basic concepts of what being a manager entails, with a brief overview of management theories. The question "What do managers actually do?" will in practice have an answer unique to each individual manager according to their skills and circumstances. The element common to all managerial roles is achieving results through other people, often, although not always, in a context of greater pressure and limited resources.

References

Dougherty, R. M. and Dougherty, A. P., 'The academic library: a time of crisis, change and opportunity', *Journal of academic librarianship*, **18** (6), 1993, 342–6

Leigh, A., *20 ways to manage better*, 2nd edn, London, Institute of Training and Development, 1995.

Peters, T. and Waterman, R., *In search of excellence*, London, Harper & Row, 1982.

Stewart, R., *The reality of organisations: a guide for managers*, 3rd edn, London, Macmillan, 1993.

Woods, M., *The new manager*, London, Element Books, 1988.

Chapter 2
Managing people

This chapter looks at:

➤ developing a systematic approach to managing library and information staff
➤ the importance of clarifying objectives and creating goals and vision
➤ motivating and supporting staff at a time of rapid change and uncertainty
➤ delegation and providing scope for personal and professional development.

Perhaps the greatest challenge for the library and information manager in the 1990s is managing and motivating staff at a time of rapid and continual change. As we saw in Chapter 1, the last 20 years have seen a major shift in thinking about management styles and the realisation of the importance of management skills. In the past, it was thought that managers either needed to be charismatic, to persuade people to do as they said, or that they should behave in an autocratic manner, leading by fear and telling their staff what to do without question or dissent. This is changing and the manager of today should be someone who is enthusiastic, persuading and motivating their staff to work as effectively as they can, often within diminishing resources.

Many writers including Tom Peters in the USA and Sir John Harvey Jones in the UK stress the importance of the people factor in the development and maintenance of successful businesses. Peters in *In search of excellence* (1982) investigated flourishing companies in the USA and suggested that staff were the most important element of an organization's success. Similarly, Sir John Harvey Jones pays tribute to the contribution made by staff in his many books and his recent TV series *Troubleshooter* and *Troubleshooter 2*.

A model of management

If managers cannot always be charismatic, what else should they be? Many writers suggest that the job of the manager is a question of balancing different needs which are sometimes in conflict. John Adair's model of **Action Centred Leadership** is useful in illustrating the three major components of the manager's role (see Figure 2.1).

Action Centred Leadership was developed in the 1970s and is, as a result, somewhat limited. For example, it ignores resources, assuming that you have the resources to achieve the task. It also presupposes an organizational logic, i.e. the manager is managed in a balanced way which does not always seem to be the case. However, it is simple and memorable – two components which are missing from many of the more complex management theories.

Adair's model is based on the premise that all managers are concerned with **achieving a task**. The task can range from something fairly straightforward such as organizing a meeting to something much more complex such as running a large library service. If resources are not available in sufficient quantity, the task may need to be modified or completed in a different way.

Adair suggests that in order to achieve the task, you need your staff or **team**. He also maintains that you should consider your staff as **individuals** – each with their own distinct combination of skills, experience and needs. It is achieving a balance between the three elements which is the mark of a good manager.

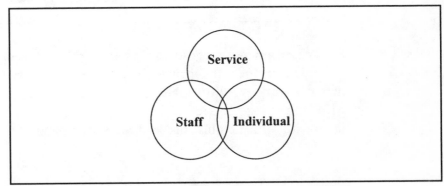

Fig. 2.1   *Action Centred Leadership model (John Adair)*

A manager hoping to develop the service, for example, should take the needs of the group and the individuals into account. The case study of the introduction of Sunday opening at Sutton's Library Service is used as an example of Action Centred Leadership.

Case study

The London Borough of Sutton's Public Library Service wished to open its libraries on Sundays as part of providing a more responsive service to residents and others. In order to see if it was feasible, a survey of users was carried out and there appeared to be a high demand. After discussion, it was decided to open the Central Library, which has a good range of services and facilities and is located in a shopping centre with a number of shops also open on Sunday.

In order to encourage staff to work on Sundays, a letter was sent to all library staff asking about their 'willingness to work'. As a result, there is a pool of staff, some of whom work most Sundays, others work the occasional day and the rest form a pool of people who can cover if there is high sickness or leave. The Sunday opening was introduced as a pilot and the use monitored for six months. The scheme has proved so popular (Sunday is now the second busiest day after Saturday) that the experiment has been made permanent and Trevor Knight, Borough Librarian of Sutton, won the Public Library Entrepreneur of the Year Award in 1995.

One by-product of the experiment is that Sunday attracts a different group of library users from those who use the libraries during the rest of the week.

Sutton's experience suggests that balancing the needs of task, team and individual can help the manager to achieve their objective. This model may not work every time, but it is a useful starting point when faced with developing a service or delivering a project. It is also useful when faced with difficult situations as discussed in Chapter 5.

Setting and agreeing goals and objectives

If management is about developing a systematic approach to achieving a complex task, there a number of important elements in this process. The first step is to set and agree goals and objectives.

Not all managers work within organizations that have clear goals and priorities. There has been a tendency, particularly in some public-sector organizations, to leave the purpose rather vague. This can create problems for staff who want some clarity about their work priorities and who would like to be able to see the end result of their work in the context of the wider organization. It can also makes it more difficult to manage the performance of individual members of staff.

The steps in managing performance are as follows:

Organization's mission
　　Department's mission and goals
　　　　Key result areas
　　　　　Unit's goals and targets
　　　　　　Individual's goals and targets
　　　　　　　Agreed yardsticks of measurement
　　　　　　　　Provide support and training
　　　　　　　　　Regular review and update

The manager's role is to help to clarify goals and expectations of staff and, according to Mabey and Iles (1994), in the context of changing circumstances, to define reality. If goals and targets do not exist at corporate level, as a manager, you may need to develop some for your own section or department. In a library context, they could be service-focused, e.g. to provide excellent service to all our customers or to ensure that we serve our customers without discrimination. They could be staff-focused, e.g. to ensure that all staff receive an induction course after two months' service or they could be outcome-focused, e.g. to raise issues by 10% within the next 12 months.

Clarifying purpose helps staff to direct their effort and energies; it also helps people to identify the priorities with their workload. Managing performance will be discussed in more detail in Chapter 5.

Staff motivation

There are hundreds of books which aim to help organizations to improve the motivation and morale of their workforce and motivation is usually a matter of considerable concern to the newly appointed or promoted managers. Motivation, however, is a very personal thing and newly appointed managers need to accept that what stimulates them will not necessarily motivate their colleagues. According to the major writers on motivation (Maslow, Herzberg, quoted in Adair, 1990) staff are motivated as much by job satisfaction, a feeling of being valued, or by opportunities for self-development, as they are by money. However, it must be said that most staff in library and information work would like to earn more as well!

Maslow's hierarchy of needs, illustrated in Figure 2.2, suggests that once our basic needs such as physiological and security needs are met, we will cease to be motivated by money or an improvement in working conditions. His view has been reinforced by Herzberg's work (both discussed in Adair, 1990) who coined the term **hygiene factors**. This suggested that problems with pay or conditions had an adverse effect on staff motivation and morale; however, once these problems had been addressed, they would not motivate positively, rather, they would cease to be an irritant or demotivator. This can be a major source of frustration to the newly appointed manager who would like to see his or her efforts recognized as well!

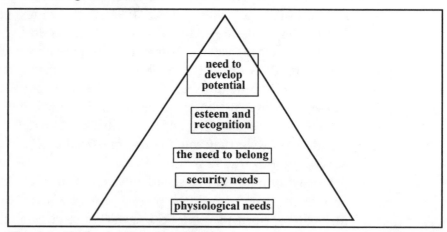

Fig. 2.2 *Maslow's hierarchy of needs*

Practical methods of motivation

Most managers feel very limited in their ability to reward and motivate their staff. Pay and conditions are generally negotiated centrally and work areas and other environmental factors are often outside the individual manager's control. However, there are a number of actions that, as a manager, you can and should take. For example, Maslow's hierarchy stresses the importance of security. Although there is no longer real job security in any sector, as a manager you can help your staff to feel more secure by providing adequate induction and on-the-job training, by communicating on a regular basis (see below, p.20), by giving praise and thanks, and helping staff to feel valued and therefore more confident. Taking staff concerns such as personal safety seriously and caring about work conditions and poor environmental circumstances do help to make staff feel that they are valued by the organization.

Managers can also help their staff to feel that they belong by encouraging staff to work as a team. Chapter 3 looks at teamwork in more detail; however, helping and encouraging staff to value each other's contribution is crucial. As it has been suggested that staff value a colleague's praise more than that of their manager, it is therefore important to create opportunities for staff to share success with their colleagues.

The fourth aspect of Maslow's hierarchy is recognition and having self-esteem. Saying thank you is an effective way of helping staff to feel that their work is useful to the organization. Saying thank you in writing and in public is also powerful, as is sharing compliments about the library and its service. Some staff may feel cynical and be overly suspicious of thanks, especially if they have had a thoughtless manager in the past, however, it is worth persevering and in time a more appreciative approach will begin to pay dividends. Put simply, making people feel that they matter is more a case of investing time rather than money!

Finally, Maslow stresses the importance of providing opportunities for self-development. If Tom Peters is correct and the future of work is about employability rather than employment, the more you can help your staff to develop their potential, the more likely they are to find rewarding work in the future. Development activities include training for new areas of responsibility; training in process skills, e.g. presentation and interpersonal skills, delegation and opportunities for job exchange and job rotation to broaden the individual's repertoire. Visits to other organizations to see how things work elsewhere, involvement in task and work groups, and opportunities to contribute to decision-making all help staff to improve their skills and confidence.

Delegation

Learning to delegate properly is an important skill which benefits you as the manager and creates learning opportunities for your staff. It an approach which helps us, as managers, to improve staff motivation and give our staff opportunities for development. It also allows us to manage our time more effectively, by ensuring that work is done at the most appropriate level. However, delegation is not an abdication of responsibility. In fact to delegate well is a challenge for most managers.

Effective delegation involves looking for opportunities to delegate and, if you can, giving the individual the whole task not just a small part of it. The dictionary defines delegation as empowering and trusting staff and that is an important prerequisite if it is to work properly. Preparation is vital. You should always allow plenty of time for briefing, training and clarifying misunderstandings. It is also important to think about realistic objectives, time scales and standards.

When delegation goes wrong, it is usually for one of two reasons. The manager delegates the job, but not the authority, i.e. the resources or power to do it properly. The second problem is unclear instructions and briefing and a reluctance to let go on behalf of the manager. Staff should also be given training and support as appropriate and priorities should be agreed to avoid conflict with other managers. It is important to monitor progress without interfering and to recognize the contribution made by public praise and thanks when the task is successfully completed. If the result is not right, the manager still retains the accountability, that is, the buck stops with you! If there is a need for negative feedback, it should be done in private and the person should be given further opportunities to develop the relevant skills. Staff will feel frustrated if they are not helped to put their new skills and experience to good use by opportunities for more interesting or rewarding work.

Other methods of motivation – coaching, staff development and training

Linked with the methods of motivation discussed above are coaching, staff development and training. In order to be truly motivated, staff need to feel that they are developing their potential. The most obvious approach is training and development activities, possibly linked to some sort of self-development profile such as that produced by the Library Association (1993). Increasingly, individuals must also be encouraged to take responsibility for their own development in partnership with their employer.

Other approaches to helping staff develop their potential include coaching, where the manager identifies the need through knowing and observing the individual's work. As a manager, you should encourage a coaching climate by getting to know the person, fostering openness and trust, providing support and giving positive and objective feedback. The coaching plan should include the results expected, the method(s) to be used and timescales to be maintained. Implementation will need a variety of approaches and, probably, the involvement of other staff if it is to work. It is also essential to review progress on a regular basis. An example of an implementation plan is illustrated in Figure 2.3.

Staff development is a vital part of helping all staff including ourselves to feel more confident and competent. As Figure 2.3. shows, there are a variety of a approaches to staff development and this topic is explored in more detail in Chapter 6.

One approach which has recently become a more popular way of supporting and developing staff is mentoring. A mentor is someone who helps an individual to manage their career by providing advice and sometimes help and guidance. Mentors are often used with newly appointed staff to help them 'learn the ropes' and are also used with positive action programmes arising out of equality of opportunity. An excellent introduction to the use of mentoring in libraries appears in Fisher (1994).

MANAGEMENT DEVELOPMENT PROGRAMME

1. Structured learning opportunities (at work)
➤ Attend a planning meeting on behalf of a senior manager
➤ Draw up a departmental budget for the first time
➤ Organize the evening cover rota
➤ Carry out staff appraisals
➤ Prepare and present a report to the senior management team.

2. On the job training
➤ Organize meetings with the finance and personnel officers as part of an extended induction programme
➤ Observe a senior management team meeting
➤ Shadow a more experienced manager.

3. Off the job training/learning opportunities
➤ Attend a seminar on budgeting and financial management
➤ Attend a conference to update information and network
➤ Attend a skills-based management development event
➤ Spend a day visiting other libraries and identify three initiatives which could act as models for your own organization
➤ Visit an exhibition and prepare a report for colleagues/senior management on possibilities for the future.
➤ Regular meeting with mentor to review progress and discuss the next stage.

Fig. 2.3 *Coaching plan for recently appointed library manager*

Different methods of motivation are shown in Figure 2.4. Spend a few minutes looking at the list and decide which rewards you can give and which are likely to be appreciated by your staff. What are you going to do about the rewards that are outside your control?

		Rewards I can give	Likely to be appreciated by the recipient
1	Praise	☐	☐
2	Gratitude – in person and in public	☐	☐
3	Interest in the individual (MBWA)	☐	☐
4	Encouragement	☐	☐
5	Induction/on the job training	☐	☐
6	Developmental training	☐	☐
7	Determine targets	☐	☐
8	Effective appraisal and follow-up	☐	☐
9	Challenging work	☐	☐
10	Being approachable	☐	☐
11	Listening and encouraging suggestions	☐	☐
12	Giving helpful feedback	☐	☐
13	A share in decision-making	☐	☐
14	More authority	☐	☐
15	Improved working conditions	☐	☐
16	Better communication	☐	☐
17	Encouraging upward communication	☐	☐
18	Encouraging job rotation; secondments	☐	☐
19	Establishing work groups with good representation	☐	☐
20	Fostering creativity and innovation	☐	☐
21	Encourage people to question established practice	☐	☐
22	Opportunity to meet with colleagues	☐	☐
23	Social events	☐	☐
24	Occasional treat	☐	☐
25	Celebrate and share success	☐	☐
26	Time off/reciprocal flexibility	☐	☐
27	Staff perks	☐	☐

Fig. 2.4 *Methods of motivation*

Communication

The third area of good people management is making a determined effort to communicate with colleagues and staff. Everyone pays lip service to the importance of communication, but few organizations invest as much time and effort in it as they should.

Stephen Covey in the *Seven habits of highly effective people* (1992) stresses the need for all managers to 'seek to understand and then be understood'. Organizations invest a lot of effort into telling staff of changes and developments, less into ensuring that the staff have really understood the message. Communication therefore needs to be more than just telling. To be effective, it should include the why as well as what, and the method of communication used should be appropriate to the needs of the audience and also allow for feedback and questions.

The principles of effective communication, whether it be to groups or individuals, are as follows. Communication should be

- clear
- correct
- concise
- courteous
- consistent.

Clarity is very important. If there is any ambiguity, confusion will result leading to incorrect or unnecessary action on the part of staff. Equally, every effort should be made to ensure that the information is correct. If not, it can have an adverse effect on the manager's credibility, leading to a lack of trust and confidence in the future. Communication should also be concise. If people are interested, supplementary information can be made available, but it is always better to work towards comprehension rather than being comprehensive. Communication should also be courteous, i.e. it should be aimed at the recipient rather than the communicator. Long words, jargon and convoluted sentences all get in the way of understanding. Finally, it should be consistent. This means that for face-to-face communication, the body language should be appropriate to the message being delivered, or, in the case of written communication, the medium should be appropriate for the content. Bad news e.g. redundancy, should always be given to the individual in private, not circulated to all and sundry in the staff newsletter!

Methods of communication

At organizational level, the following can be useful, especially at a time of major change.

➤ Top manager roadshows and information briefings. These are led by management, provide an opportunity to clarify what is happening and why, and perhaps, as important, allow staff to ask questions and clarify concerns.

➤ Telephone hotlines are used by large organizations such as BT and Westminster City Council during times of major change. They allow staff to express fears and concerns and also provide management with a summary of where further effort on communication might be useful.

➤ Corporate or departmental newsletters are another approach used by many organizations. The format and content depends on the purpose, but does allow correct information to be circulated to all staff. There is however, usually a delay in the information being available and newsletters can be seen as a management mouthpiece if they are too complementary.

➤ Briefing sheets and updates can help to fill these gaps, especially if they are faxed or e-mailed to recipients. They allow management to respond to the questions and concerns which emerge during any period of change and have an intrinsic urgency due to the mode of distribution.

➤ Change is an unsettling time when procedures and routines may lapse. Circulating instructions and procedures to remind staff of important tasks and routines can help to maintain order and define the new approach.

➤ Employee surveys and feedback can be helpful in ascertaining where there are fears and misunderstandings. However, surveying staff at a time when change and uncertainty are afoot will not result in many positive responses. Use this approach only if you are prepared to hear and act on the results!

> Finally, opportunities to share success are an important part of any communication strategy. They help to create a sense of pride in the organization and allow staff to reflect on the positive as well as the problems. They can also help to counter-balance the uncertainty and cynicism mentioned above.

Team briefing

At local team level, communication needs to be a regular event with an emphasis on local matters and more personal matters as well as corporate ones. A well-established method of regular communication is team briefing which has been developed and pioneered by the Industrial Society. Team briefing involves regular meetings between the manager and their staff. They provide an opportunity for the manager to inform their staff of matters relating to their work as well as information about the organization itself. If handled correctly, they should also enable staff to ask questions and express concerns which can then be responded to at the next meeting.

The usual pattern for a team briefing is as follows:

> **Progress** – information about positive developments at local and corporate level. Items can include information such as updates on the budget and income generation; reports on new business, increased use of the service or details of a new location.
> **Policy** – changes in how things are to be done and how this will affect everyone. Examples include new procedures for booking leave; sickness reporting etc.
> **People** – a chance to welcome and introduce new staff or give best wishes to those about to leave; discussion on changes to people's jobs, e.g. acting arrangements and an opportunity to share team and individual successes.
> **Points for action** – things that need to be done before the next meeting – arrange a visit; organize new publicity etc. A note should be made of the task and the person responsible and then circulated to everyone present to act as a reminder.

For team briefings to work, they must be held on a regular basis, at least monthly is preferred. It is important for them to be systematic, e.g. in the Industrial Society, the briefing always takes place at 09.30 on the first Monday of the month. They should also be face to face and led by the line manager and the subjects (see above) must be relevant to the needs of the team. Finally, they should be brief, no more than one hour in length. If there is too much information to cover, it is better to make the briefings more frequent than to make them too long.

Team meetings

Team meetings are another approach to communicating with staff. They differ from team briefings in that they are more concerned with specific problems rather than being a channel for regular communication. For team meetings to be effective, they should be timed to allow the optimum number of staff to attend. They should also have an agenda which gives sufficient detail for the topic(s) under discussion to be clear. Incidentally, it has been found that agendas that contain questions, e.g. 'How are we going to spend this year's staff development budget?', seem to elicit more responses than topics. The agenda should always be circulated well in advance and allow time for the participants to prepare adequately, including canvassing colleagues if that is appropriate and within the members' responsibility.

Meetings' skills are increasingly important for everyone at work, whatever their level, and as a good manager, you should encourage your staff to make contributions and suggestions. Again, depending on the complexity of the matters to be discussed at the meeting, it may be necessary to limit the number of items covered and the time available, and if necessary to agree priorities at the meeting. A good manager will also summarize key decisions so that everyone is clear on the way forward. It is essential to circulate an action list and follow it up at the next meeting, otherwise things will not get done and the group will waste time going over old ground. Other methods for encouraging team communications include informal methods such as brown bag lunches or exchange of experience sessions. *Communications for managers* (Industrial Society, 1994) includes useful advice and examples on a variety of methods of communication.

Face-to-face communication

As a manager, the most important aspect of communication, is from you to individual members of your staff. Informal communication reinforces the importance of the individual and their specific contribution to the delivery of the service. It also provides an opportunity to help people to feel they belong.

The benefits of one-to-one (1:1) communication are as follows:

➤ talking to staff helps them to understand why changes or developments are being proposed;

➤ it helps you to gauge response to your ideas and suggestions and helps to warn you of opposition and perhaps, to avoid conflict;

➤ you get to know your staff and their aptitudes and interests and it enables you to take an interest in and appreciate their work;

➤ perhaps most importantly, it allows you to listen to their ideas and suggestions and to ascertain where they feel they need help and support.

The rule of thumb for personal contact with staff is as follows:

➤ At least **once a day,** see all those who **report** directly to you

➤ At least **once a week,** see all those who **contribute** directly to your objectives

➤ At least **once a month,** see all who make an **indirect contribution** to your objectives (O'Reilly, 1993).

In the case of multi-site operation, meeting face to face on a daily basis may be unrealistic. However, keeping in regular contact by telephone, fax or e-mail is important, as is visiting whenever possible.

Methods of communication with individuals

➤ Staff appraisal or performance and development reviews provide an opportunity to meet with staff on a 1:1 basis to discuss their work and achievements. However, as appraisal is normally carried out on an annual or even two-yearly basis, on its own, it is not frequent enough to be a really effective method of keeping in touch.

➤ One-to-one meetings are becoming increasingly popular. Usually held weekly or fortnightly, they allow you to keep in touch with your staff and their work. However, in order to be really effective, both sides should prepare properly and your role is to listen rather than talk. The 1:1 has sometimes become an occasion when the manager loads even more work on their staff and then berates them for not coping well with what they have already!

➤ Management by walking about is a technique endorsed by Peters and Waterman in *In search of excellence*. It involves you as the manager visiting and talking to staff at their place of work rather than expecting them to always come to you. MBWA as it is known, is about taking an interest in staff and their work and links with the methods of motivation described above.

Whichever technique is used, the most important skill when meeting with staff on a 1:1 basis is the ability to listen. It is perhaps well to remember that people talk even if you don't listen, but they talk to each other, their friends and families and, if they are feeling really fed up, your customers. Listening demonstrates value and respect for staff; it is a vehicle for change and it helps you to reward victories and implement change decisions.

Effective listening

The principles of effective listening are as follows:

➤ You should stop talking and start listening. We have two ears and one mouth and should try to use them in that proportion.

➤ As the manager, you should try to put the other person at their ease and show them that you want to listen by using eye contact, paying attention and asking questions.

➤ Remember also that talking to managers can be daunting for many staff and you may have to persevere to get a good response.

➤ Always try to minimize distractions, give the person your full attention and give them time to say what they want.

➤ You need to be patient and try not to interrupt. You must also suspend judgment and go easy on argument or criticism. 'Yes and' rather than 'yes but' is the best response. (Incidentally, do not criticize staff for understanding less than you about the work situation. You are in a position to be better informed.)

➤ Also remember that praise does wonders for people's sense of hearing!

➤ Summarize what you have heard to ensure that there is no confusion or misunderstanding.

➤ Finally, if you have promised to act on something, make sure you do!

Other approaches which can encourage feedback from staff include:

➤ Quality circles and focus groups
➤ Suggestions schemes
➤ Innovative ideas schemes/awaydays
➤ Brainstorming sessions.

Again, the Industrial Society's *Communication for managers* (1994) provides useful ideas and suggestions.

Finally, in this section, perhaps the best advice a manager can have in motivating his or her staff is as follows:

The **six** most important words	'I admit I made a mistake'
The **five** most important words	'You did a good job'
The **four** most important words	'What do you think?'
The **three** most important words	'Let's work together'
The **two** most important words	'Thank you'
The **one** most important word	'You'

Summary

For you to be a successful manager, you must be able to manage people effectively. There is no single blueprint, which if adopted will guarantee you success. Rather, there is a range of skills and techniques covering motivation, delegation, staff development, communication and listening. This chapter has provided you with an 'artist's palette' of examples of good practice in these areas. It is for you as the manager to select the approaches you feel comfortable with and which are relevant in your own role. The key action is then to adapt these techniques and make them work for you in your own personal style. You should also consider the need for having more than one fixed style – the adaptable manager may resemble a chameleon, exhibiting different styles to cope with different situations.

References

Adair, J., *Action centred leadership*, London, Gower, 1990a.

Adair, J., *Understanding motivation*, London, Talbot Adair, 1990b.

Belasco, J. A., *Teaching the elephant to dance*, London, Century Business, 1990.

Covey, S., *The seven habits of highly effective people*, Berkeley, California, Simon and Schuster, 1992.

Fisher, B., *Mentoring*, London, Library Association Publishing, 1994.

Industrial Society, *Communications for managers*, London, Industrial Society, 1994.

Library Association, *CPD framework*, London, LA, 1993.

Mabey, C. and Iles, P., *Managing learning*, Milton Keynes, Open University, 1994.

O' Riley, P., *The skills development handbook for busy managers*, London, McGraw-Hill, 1993.

Peters, T., *In search of excellence*, London, Harper & Row, 1982.

Chapter 3
Managing effective teams

This chapter looks at:

➤ what constitutes an effective team
➤ the stages of team development
➤ management skills for teamwork
➤ helping teams to be productive
➤ dealing with difficulties.

The third component of Adair's model concerns the team and its importance in achieving a balance between the needs of the staff and service. This is echoed by writers such as Tom Peters who see the team as being the focal point of organizations in the future.

Teamwork has become increasingly important in all organizations including libraries, because the delivery of such services has become more complex, particularly in the light of limited and diminishing resources. Teamwork also provides the social interaction which most of us need to create that sense of belonging and, according to Meredith Belbin (1993), although an individual cannot be perfect a team can be. However, the skilled team does not happen automatically and developing and maintaining a truly effective team is one of the biggest challenges facing every manager.

Components of an effective team

A team is usually defined as 'a group of people working towards a common objective' and the characteristics of the effective team are as follows. There should be:

➤ a shared sense of purpose and clear goals and objectives;

➤ good use of the team's resources, including opportunities for individual development and opportunities to satisfy our need to 'belong';

➤ a choice of team work or individual action whichever is more appropriate and a balance in skills, experience and team roles;

➤ leadership that is effective in balancing the needs of the task with those of the team and is confident and credible in representing the team to the outside world;

➤ honest, open communication and courtesy between members;

➤ an understanding of team processes and possibly, an agreed code of conduct;

➤ procedures (e.g. regular team meetings and briefings), which help to guide the team so that it achieves its targets;

➤ effective approaches to problem-solving, decision-making and conflict resolution as well as the confidence to experiment and take risks (within reason);

➤ finally, a willingness to review and learn from experience.

According to Radl, 'A team should be homogeneous enough to ensure stability . . . (yet) heterogeneous enough to ensure variety, creativity and avoid complacency'. Radl's quote illustrates one of the real challenges of developing an effective team. The group needs to have enough in common to create a cohesion, but it should also be sufficiently diverse to represent a range of views and to avoid complacency. The current tendency is for teams to become more varied which reflects the changing nature of organizations but also the increasing complexity of the task. Few teams consist of people with similar qualifications, backgrounds and experience; today's team is diverse, it is likely to be together for a limited time and therefore poses an even greater challenge for you as the manager.

Stages of team development

Understanding how teams function help you to create a more effective team. Tuckman (quoted in Fraser and Neville, 1993) suggests that every team goes through a series of stages. These are usually called forming, storming, norming and performing and the characteristics of each stage are shown below.

1 **Forming or undeveloped phase**
   ➤ Predominately task-centred.
   ➤ Confusion over purpose, participants are anxious and apprehensive.
   ➤ Goals need to be defined.
   ➤ There is low conflict, but possible 'bids' for leadership.
   ➤ Can be an anxious time for everyone and particularly frustrating for those who are task-focused.

2 **Storming or experimental phase**
   ➤ Predominately individual focus – emphasis on the word 'I'.
   ➤ There is increased conflict over goals and the way of working.
   ➤ As the group becomes more familiar, individuals become less tolerant of each other and can become competitive.
   ➤ The group will need process skills as well as task skills if it is to succeed.

3 **Norming or consolidating phase**
   ➤ This is where you should begin to see a team focus and the use of the word 'We'.
   ➤ Information and ideas start to be shared and the group has a greater ability to resolve conflict through give and take.
   ➤ Participants are more willing to experiment and disclose information about themselves.
   ➤ However, there can be a development of group norms which become hostile to 'mavericks' or those who do not 'fit' for whatever reason.

4 **Performing or mature phase**
   ➤ This is where the task, team and individual needs are in balance.
   ➤ There is a sense of purpose and direction and good communication and trust between members.
   ➤ Problem solving and decision making are good and the group is able to resolve conflict.
   ➤ However, there is a danger of 'groupthink', i.e. members are reluctant to challenge the group even where it is justified. The team can

also become complacent, intolerant of 'outsiders' and form cliques which affect its ability to work with other groups or teams.

Each stage of teamwork will need different leadership skills. The manager's role in helping his or her team through these stages will change. Hershey and Blanchard (also quoted in Fraser and Neville, 1993) built on Tuckman's work and suggested that there are four leadership styles which overlap the four stages (see Figure 3.1).

➤ TELL
➤ SELL
➤ CONSULT
➤ PARTICIPATE

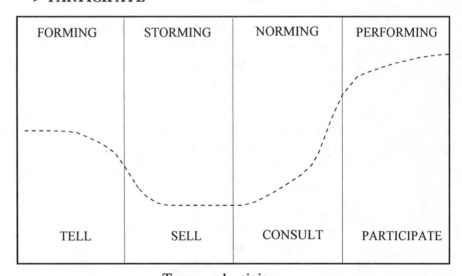

Fig. 3.1 *Teamwork model*

In order to progress your team between these different stages, as the manager, you have a vital role in supporting and directing their work. For example, at the forming stage, it will be important to:

➤ Help staff get to know each other and their individual contribution to the task

31

➤ Provide a sense of purpose and clarify limits, deadlines and constraints
➤ Assess the skills balance and try to identify team roles
➤ Begin to anticipate likely blocks and barriers to progress.

At the storming stage, the manager has a particularly delicate role. You should try to:

➤ Continue to provide direction
➤ Encourage a sense of trust and openness (not always easy)
➤ Handle conflict positively and look for common ground
➤ Be prepared to mediate and determine a way forward which might not be popular with everyone.

At the norming stage, the group is more mature and some of the negative behaviours experienced earlier should have dwindled. As the manager, your role is to become less directive and more supportive and includes:

➤ Maintaining openness and trust
➤ Challenging the group if they start to become complacent
➤ Celebrating individual and team success
➤ Encouraging a regular review to ensure that the team is staying on track.

Finally, at the performing stage, your role is to:

➤ Lead from behind
➤ Ensure that the team has the resources and the support they need
➤ Represent the team to the wider organization
➤ Encourage regular evaluation to avoid complacency and learning from experience.

Team composition

Few managers are able to appoint their own teams from scratch. They are much more likely to inherit at least half of the members or an established team. As well as skills and experience, each of these individuals will have a preference for one or more team 'roles'. Understanding this element can help you to develop a more productive team.

The work of Meredith Belbin

The concept of team roles was developed by Meredith Belbin in the 1980s (Belbin, 1981). Working at Henley Management College, he suggested that an effective team needed a series of roles to be represented if it was to be successful. He proposed that there are nine team roles. Some focus on the achievement of the task, while others contribute to the working of the team. According to Belbin, every role is crucial to the effective operation of any team. Table 3.1 illustrates Belbin's team roles.

Table 3.1 Belbin's team roles

Team role	Positive qualities	Allowable weaknesses
Shaper	Task centred Channels energies Helps to get task underway	Prone to irritation and impatience Can be off-putting to others
Chair	Balances task and team needs Recognizes individual strengths and maximizes the contribution of everyone	Not always creative Can appear to be manipulative
Plant	Creative and unorthodox Helps to see alternative approaches Imaginative and knowledgeable	Not always very practical Tendency to be intolerant of those who are less creative
Resource investigator	Makes links with external contacts Willing to explore and develop new ideas Responds well to challenge	Loses interest easily May need to be 'kept on track'
Implementer	Turns ideas into practicalities Carried out agreed plans systematically Well-organized, hardworking and efficient	Not always responsive to new ideas Can seem to be inflexible

continued overleaf

Team worker	Supports team members Builds on suggestions and keeps team functioning Promotes 'esprit de corps'	May be indecisive at a time of crisis
Monitor/ evaluator	Analyses problems, evaluates ideas and suggestions Helps the team to take balanced decisions Good judgment	May lack inspiration May not inspire others
Completer/ finisher	Ensures nothing has been overlooked Maintains a sense of urgency Enables the team to follow through	Perfectionist Reluctant to let go Worries about small details
Specialist	Single-minded Provides specialist know- ledge	Tends to talk in jargon Contributes on a narrow front

Belbin's work is useful in analysing whether a team is balanced, although he is not suggesting that all teams must consist of nine members. Some writers question whether Belbin's work has any relevance at all to those working in libraries and information units. Robert Bluck (1995), for example, reports that Belbin's findings work best when a team is selected for a specific project and all members have equal status. He suggests that Belbin should be used with extreme caution in a library context. However, if a team is not working as well as it could, analysing the roles played by individual members may identify 'gaps' and enable you, as the manager, to take steps to alleviate the problems.

Task/team skills

As well as thinking about leadership styles and individual roles, any team needs a balance of skills if it is to be effective. The trick in team work is to balance the needs of task and team.

Exercise 3.1

Spend ten minutes writing a list of behaviours which

(a) help to achieve the task; and
(b) help to build the team.

Better still, get your staff to do this in pairs or small groups.

Then ask them to identify the behaviours which hinder effective team work. Use their ideas to generate a discussion about your own team and how it might be more effective in the future.

Some ideas are as follows:

Behaviours which help to achieve the task

> ➤ Initiating ideas
> ➤ Giving opinions
> ➤ Producing information, data and statistics
> ➤ Asking for information, ideas and suggestions
> ➤ Defining problems and suggesting solutions
> ➤ Organizing and agreeing procedures and deciding priorities
> ➤ Checking for understanding, agreement and disagreement
> ➤ Maintaining direction and keeping time
> ➤ Summarizing and clarifying.

Behaviours which help to strengthen the team

> ➤ Patience!
> ➤ Empathy
> ➤ Listening and encouraging contributions to ensure equal participation
> ➤ Giving verbal and non-verbal support
> ➤ Mediating – looking for common ground
> ➤ Defusing conflict and keeping things positive
> ➤ Reducing tension/using humour – sometimes!
> ➤ Complimenting and reconciling differences by looking for an acceptable way forward.

Behaviours that weaken a team and inhibit its effectiveness

➤ Aggression
➤ Competition
➤ Destructive criticism or sarcasm
➤ Withdrawal
➤ Disapproval
➤ Impatience.

Encouraging creativity in teams

Many teams get distracted by detail and fail to be sufficiently creative. Encouraging creativity in teams is important and there are a number of approaches which can help you to do this. Wish listing, for example, helps to break the cycle of low expectations and achievement and can be useful in stimulating ideas. It is a technique which can also be helpful in reaching agreement where there are different views. Other approaches include **brainstorming** which encourages staff to work as a group to generate as many ideas as possible without judgement or evaluation. The theory is that quantity will lead to quality. Brainwriting is a variation on this and involves individuals writing ideas/suggestions in response to a problem. These ideas are then circulated to provide inspiration for others to add to or amend. **Brainwriting** is more private than brainstorming and therefore useful where there is a reluctance to disclose information or where staff work at distant locations. It also lends itself to e-mail approaches

Developing codes of conduct is another approach, mainly used by the commercial sector, to assist teams to be more effective. The code clarifies the behaviour which is (and is not) acceptable at team meetings and helps to balance different needs. An example of a code of conduct from BT is shown in Figure 3.2.

> **CODE OF CONDUCT**
> ➤We respect one another
> ➤We work as a team
> **Meetings groundrules**
> ➤Only one person to speak at a time
> ➤Strive for agreement or at least a way forward
> ➤Listen and share responsibility
> ➤No, or limited, AOB items
> ➤Keep to time

Fig. 3.2 *Sample code of conduct*

Managing team performance and productivity

Another difficulty with managing teams is keeping them on track, i.e. ensuring that they meet their deadlines. Project-planning techniques are useful in maintaining progress and in identifying where slippage may occur.

Methods for keeping teams on track

Planning

➤ establish clear objectives for **all** concerned
➤ ensure that everyone knows what is expected from them and who is responsible for doing what.

Plan for the achievement of the objectives

➤ use project control and monitoring techniques to identify the components of the task
➤ determine milestones; standards and accountabilities (an example is shown over the page)
➤ anticipate problems and try to identify options if things start to slip
➤ be prepared to revise timescales or outcomes if necessary.

Make sure the task stays on track

➤ check regularly with stakeholders or sponsors of the project
➤ circulate regular updates on progress to all concerned
➤ monitor progress for early warning of delays or problems and chase as necessary.

Maintain quality

➤ set appropriate standards and lead by example
➤ specify quality standards from others involved – both internal and external
➤ tackle problems of poor delivery as soon as possible.

Keep the 'team' motivated

➤ hold regular meetings and reports on progress which include new and 'invisible' members
➤ encourage an early warning system and **do not** shoot the messenger!
➤ maintain your own vision and enthusiasm.

Review and learn

➤ encourage the group to reflect on the task and how the team worked
➤ note problems and take steps to prevent them happening next time.

One difficulty with keeping teams on track is the complexity of the work and the potential for confusion to occur. There are a number of approaches which help to ensure that deadlines and responsibilities are clear. The bar or GANTT charts (Figures 3.3 and 3.4) are common in project planning and can be useful to show deadlines and milestones.

	Feb.	Mar.	Apr.	May	June	July
Activity						
1. Draft ideas to be developed	▨					
2. Article for March newsletter	▨					
3. Deadline for final programme		▨				
4. Publicity to printing		▨				
5. Distribute information to all staff			▨			
6. Article for June newsletter				▨		
7. Final arrangements for bookings and logistics					▨	
8. Conference fortnight					▨	
9. Final debrief and action planning						▨

Fig. 3.3 *Sample project plan for conference organization*

	Week 2	Week 4	Week 8	Week 12	Week 16
Call for project proposal	▨				
Prepare project proposal and acceptance		▨			
Undertake literature review			M ▨		
Meet project sponsor			▨		
Pilot and circulate questionnaire			M		
Research and draft report				M ▨	
Presentation to sponsor					▨

M = milestone or important deadline

Fig. 3.4 *Barchart example: sample research project*

It can also be useful to specify who is designated to complete aspects of the task. A responsibility matrix (Table 3.2), can help us to clarify responsibilities and ensure that everyone knows what is expected from them.

Table 3.2 Responsibility matrix

	Prepare project proposal/ tender	*Undertake literature review and pilot questionnaire*	*Draft report and amend as necessary*	*Agree with project sponsor*
PEOPLE				
Jane (project manager)	S		S	RD
Jill (researcher)	RD	RD	A	
Jack(researcher)		A	RD	
John (sponsor)				S

Key: **R** Responsible for
        D Doing
        A Assisting
        S Signing off

Problems with teams

Finally, many managers, those who are established as well as recently appointed, are concerned about how to deal with problems in teams. Most teams go wrong because the task/team balance is not achieved. With some teams it is ingrained individualism and competitiveness, while others indulge in 'scapegoating' i.e. blaming one individual (usually someone who is different) for all the group's woes.

Practical ideas which can help us to avoid and tackle problems

Ingrained individualism and competition

> ➤ encourage working co-operatively to 'beat' the external competition (a common enemy often works wonders in pulling a group together!)
> ➤ reiterate the purpose of the team
> ➤ ensure quick success through short-scale, achievable projects/milestones.

Scapegoating

> ➤ emphasize the importance of everyone's contribution and tackle problems **early.** Stephen Covey's book has some excellent examples of the need to value everyone's contribution (Covey, 1992).

Lack of team communications

> ➤ emphasize the importance of keeping in touch with each other as well as the team leader
> ➤ encourage and provide regular updates on progress
> ➤ allow the group to ask questions and 'challenge' (constructively), the way things are done.

Trouble between individual team members

> ➤ anticipate difficulties – ask 'what if' questions
> ➤ use 'diplomatic confrontation' to bring the differences out into the open
> ➤ attack the problem not the people
> ➤ acknowledge the difficulties and encourage everyone to work towards a solution.

Summary

Developing teams is crucial to success. From this chapter you should now be able to identify what constitutes an effective team and also understand the principal stages of team development. You should now think about your own team(s) and analyse the behaviours and skills they exhibit. This chapter has sought to identify examples of positive and negative behaviours in teams and also to suggest practical methods for managing and maintaining high team performance in the context of a complex interaction of individual behaviours, attitudes and performance levels. A team requires supportive management, a sense of direction and needs to be led by example. You should now be able to identify the actions you need to take to ensure your team(s) are high performers.

References

Belbin, M., *Management teams: why they fail*, London, Butterworth Heinemann, 1981.

Belbin, M., *Team roles at work*, London Butterworth Heinemann, 1993

Bluck, R., *Team management*, London, Library Association Publishing, 1995.

Fraser, A. and Neville, S., *Teambuilding*, London, Industrial Society, 1993.

Industrial Society, *Communications for managers*, London, Industrial Society, 1994.

Chapter 4
Delivering quality library services

This chapter looks at:

➤ the pressure on libraries to deliver quality services
➤ different approaches to managing quality
➤ determining our customers' needs through surveys and other approaches
➤ managing customers' expectations through statements and charters of service and developing targeted services linked to customers' needs
➤ the management of quality and performance – process and people.

One of the key developments in the last fifteen years has been the increased interest in quality and quality assurance. In the 1980s, many commercial organizations adopted quality processes to improve their competitiveness and a number of different approaches are now in use.

What is quality and why is it important?

What is quality and what is the point of it? Library and information managers are under considerable pressure to deliver quality services. This arises out of an increased awareness of the cost of services in all sectors and a need to demonstrate value for money. Quality services are not a luxury, they are essential for our survival. In addition, the quality approach should save money by eliminating mistakes and leading to the adoption of the most efficient and effective processes. It should also provide better clarity about what is, and is not, expected from the service, helping us to anticipate and avoid problems and giving us better relationships with our customers

As individuals, developing quality processes should give us more control over our work and, therefore, improved time management. It can also provide more job satisfaction and opportunities for personal development. Finally, external validation, e.g. through recognition by professional or funding bodies or public accreditation through the granting of the Charter Mark or other quality award, can be motivating for staff and demonstrates to your 'public' that the service you provide is recognized as being excellent.

Philip Crosby, one of the major writers in the field of quality, defines it as a 'journey not a destination' (1984). This is a crucial point as one of the most important elements of quality is continuous improvement. If we recognize that our customers and the context within which we work are constantly changing, it becomes essential that our services respond to these new challenges. Similarly, it is important that the approach to quality which we adopt is appropriate to these circumstances.

The major components of a quality approach are as follows:

➤ **Clarity**	**Say** what you are going to do
➤ **Conformance**	**Do** what you **say** you are going to do
➤ **Consistency**	Get it **right first time**, every time and do it the **same** for every customer and at every location
➤ **Confirmation**	**Demonstrate** that you have done it
➤ **Continuous improvement**	Do it **again**, but **better each time**

Crosby also suggests that the biggest barrier to quality is complacency, the assumption that our customers are captive and there is no need to improve what we do or how we do it.

Approaches to developing quality

ISO 9000

One well-established approach to demonstrating quality is to gain the ISO 9000 standard, previously BS 5750, a recognized quality accreditation system. A number of library and information units have gained recognition under this scheme, including the University of Central Lancashire, Building Design Partnership and Sandwell College. Others, for example, the Ministry of Defence, are working towards accreditation to demonstrate a consistent and acceptable approach. The British Standards Institution which accredits the scheme expects the organization to develop a quality control system which ensures a consistency across the service and to different customers and is complied with by staff. It also identifies the notion of 'fitness for purpose', i.e. the service is appropriate to and meets the needs of the customers.

Many libraries have developed a staff manual to assist in delivering quality services. However, these can easily become out of date, covered with scribbled amendments to suit local circumstances and are not always subject to regular and managed updating. Under the British Standards' approach, the quality manual becomes an official document, amendments are controlled and only distributed to recognized managers and it is expected that everyone will abide by it. (If there is non-conformance, the reasons and the discrepancy are also noted.)

The British Standards approach has been subject to recent criticism in that some organizations which have achieved recognition have not always been seen to be customer-driven. However, according to Peter Brophy of the University of Central Lancashire, which achieved recognition in 1994, it does help to contribute to a quality culture within the library service. It also recognizes the importance of all staff in developing and auditing the standards that are set as well as presenting a powerful message to the organization that quality matters (Brophy, 1994). Ellis and Norton (1993) provide a useful overview of the application of the British Standards approach to library and information units.

Total Quality Management

The more common approach to developing quality in libraries and information units has been the adoption of Total Quality Management or TQM as it is better known. TQM involves staff understanding their role in delivering quality through clarifying what is expected of them. In addition, it is important to foster a management approach which empowers and motivates. Andrew Forrest (1994), describes the difference between an ordinary approach to service where staff have no authority to make decisions and the TQM approach where staff can do anything (within reason) to please the customer.

In a library context, TQM involves:

➤ ascertaining customers' needs through surveys, focus groups and other approaches and monitoring their satisfaction with the services provided

➤ identifying where there are blocks and barriers to quality through analysis of problems

➤ developing programmes to improve quality at a variety of levels including customer care training, which includes dealing with 'difficult' customers

➤ encouraging suggestions and comments from customers – positive as well as negative and responding to these

➤ training for managers in delivering quality services

➤ quality circles or task groups to encourage staff to identify problems and propose solutions for dealing with these

➤ quality manuals and guidelines for staff to clarify what is required, without providing a blueprint which covers every eventuality.

Developing a customer-focused service

Determining customers' needs

Libraries are putting considerable effort and energy into ascertaining customers' needs. This is partly to ensure that the service becomes as responsive as possible, but also to provide numerical and anecdotal evidence which might be needed in the age of increased accountability and to justify bids for resources.

Some questions concerning **customers** which managers may choose to consider are:

➤ Who are they and what do they do?

➤ What about potential customers, those who leave and lapsed customers?

➤ Where do they come from, what do they know about the services the organization/institution provides and how do they find out about changes in service?

➤ What services do they use, and when, and how much?

➤ What is the **appropriate** 'level' (or quality) of service required?

➤ What services do they need which are currently **not** provided?

➤ What services are currently provided but are no longer needed?

➤ What are customer perceptions of the service, e.g. image, customer-friendly, value-for-money?

➤ What 'competition' exists and what alternative sources do customers actually use?

➤ How much are customers prepared to pay for basic/value added services?

➤ What are the customers key quality criteria?

➤ How well does the service actually meet these criteria and how satisfied is the customer?

➤ Does the service delivered actually match customer **expectations**?

Making links with our customers

In order to answer the questions posed above, libraries across the sectors have developed a range of both formal and informal mechanisms for getting customer feedback on the services provided, e.g. via library committees in the academic sector. Many libraries will serve a number of different groups of customers, not all of whom will have the same agenda, making a consensus difficult to achieve. In many cases, creating the opportunity for customers to voice their comments and concerns is the key action. It sends the message that this service is willing and prepared to listen and helps you, as the manager, to define priorities for service development.

In managing the process of making (and maintaining) links with customers, the key objectives are to:

1. identify existing, potential (and possibly, lapsed) customers.
2. ensure that the importance of 'the customer' is communicated to everyone involved; recognize that everyone has customers and the internal customer is often the key to our success; according to Hopson and Scally (1989), 'If you are not serving a customer, you are serving someone who is'.
3. keep customers informed, especially if things go wrong or there is a delay.

4. create a personal relationship and/or a partnership with your customers.

5. establish and maintain a two-way flow of communication/information.

A number of libraries have developed a wide variety of interesting and practical ways of making and maintaining links with their customers. As a manager you should assess the method(s) appropriate to your circumstances. The following should provide some ideas:

➤ Nominating a specific liaison person(s) to act as the focus for customers. Make them known and encourage contact in whatever way is suitable – by personal contact, phone, e-mail or fax.

➤ Holding regular meetings with customers (at times convenient for them).

➤ Representing library interests within the organization's formal decision-making meetings or committees and also contributing to the debate on wider issues.

➤ Personal informal contact . . . in the lift, the corridor, the tea bar etc.

➤ Visiting them . . . 'Walking the customer'. Sadly, too few managers/staff leave their own domain to visit customers in their workplace whether it is their office or laboratory or the 'shop-floor'.

➤ Establishing customer forums/focus groups or interview sessions.

➤ Holding open days or open sessions, possibly around the launch of new services. To avoid the possibility of a thin attendance be explicit about the specific benefits involved for individuals (and possibly include a glass of wine!).

➤ Targeting specific communities or customer groups.

➤ Producing clear and explicit professional publicity and information material in the form of guides, bookmarks, displays, newsletters, posters and their equivalent in electronic format.

➤ Establishing charters or codes of practice which clarify what your service does and does not do. They can also help you to clarify the responsibilities of your customers.

➤ Introducing comment and feedback cards (including electronic bulletin boards) to encourage customers to express their opinions both 'good' and 'bad'. The card in use at the BBC phrases it thus:

'Tell us what we're doing right/Tell us where we could improve'. The latter statement sent a powerful message to both staff and customers, i.e. that you want to use the customers' comments to improve services, not to attribute blame. There is no mention of the word 'complaint' which can have a negative and demotivating connotation.

➤ In larger organizations, making 0800 telephone numbers or helplines available. Customers who contact you are less likely to 'vote with their feet'.

➤ Conducting surveys of customer needs (by various means available, e.g. printed, e-mail, electronic, telephone).

➤ Determining customer satisfaction measures (including exit interviews) and suggestion schemes for customers and staff.

➤ Developing innovative approaches to encouraging feedback. Lewisham Libraries, for example, have introduced a videobox which enables customers to make a three-minute video on their views of the service. In academic libraries, notice-boards have encouraged students to provide positive and negative comments about the service.

➤ Electronic/online approaches, e.g. Libra produced by Priority Search Ltd.

Structured interviews as a means of gaining feedback

Structured interviews can be a particularly useful way of obtaining qualitative data about customer views of the library. One approach taken by a well-established academic library was to conduct a series of sessions with a wide range of students to determine their library and information needs with a particular emphasis on information skills support. The method adopted involved using a number of semi-structured interviews with an external facilitator to ensure an acceptable measure of consistency across the various groups of volunteers. The key points were to:

➤ provide an independent and open-minded facilitator who does not distort or judge the views expressed.

➤ clearly define the areas to be addressed at the outset.

➤ gather a representative sample of volunteers for interview; the number of people is likely to be a small percentage of the total customer base, typically 5%, nevertheless, with care, the sample can (and should) include all important groups and shades of opinion.

➤ limit each session to 6–8 individuals to ensure that the whole group, not just the vociferous individual(s), are involved.

➤ provide a relaxing conducive environment, with set start and finish times.

➤ establish ground rules of confidentiality and explain how the outcome of the interviews will be of benefit to the individual and the organization.

➤ tease out all shades of opinion; remember that if consensus is reached, it will be the exception rather than the rule!

➤ whoever facilitates the discussion should be prepared, with an interview structure; this should include a range of 'trigger' questions rather than a rigid script.

➤ ensure that notes (or possibly a flip-chart) are used to record the discussion, and that the principal issues, solutions and problems are summarized.

➤ the session should be analysed, the report written promptly and provision made for access to the report/outcomes to the interviewees.

The structured interview has the merit of involving volunteers for in-depth discussion and gives them the opportunity to express opinions in a non-threatening environment. Although finding a truly representative sample may be daunting, this approach can overcome the tendency towards 'questionnaire fatigue' where customers can become tired of receiving questionnaires through the post or being accosted in the high street and asked for their opinions.

Community profiling

Another approach which has been common in commercial and public libraries for two decades and is now being adapted for academic libraries is community profiling. The community profile carried out an in-depth look at a user community – its demographics, age profile, interests and likely needs. One university has carried out community profiles of its students using the following headings:

Analysis of course data

> ➤ statistical information – age, gender, ethnic origin, etc.
> ➤ mode of attendance – full time, part time, distance learning, other, e.g. weekend
> ➤ level – undergraduate, postgraduate, research
> ➤ teaching and learning methods.

Some useful sources

> ➤ prospectus, syllabus, unit guides
> ➤ course monitoring reports and validation reports
> ➤ project work and assignments
> ➤ feedback from formal course/departmental meetings.

Interviews with relevant staff to ascertain needs and difficulties experienced

> ➤ course tutors, admission tutors, liaison officers
> ➤ student representatives.

Benchmark; using evidence from elsewhere, where appropriate

> ➤ literature searching and keeping up to date
> ➤ networks/SCONUL/COFHE groups etc.
> ➤ 'league tables' – the consistent approach via 'the Effective Academic Library'.

Surveys of users

> ➤ define needs and test assumptions
> ➤ satisfaction surveys.

Analysis of statistical/management information

> ➤ gate figures and patterns of use
> ➤ loan statistics
> ➤ interlibrary loans
> ➤ other relevant data consistent with 'the Effective Academic Library'.

As a result of carrying out the community profile, the service has been adapted to suit the needs of particular student groups.

Other aspects of developing quality services

Managing expectations

One aspect of developing quality which has become more common is to seek to manage customers' expectations and match the delivery of the service to these. In libraries, the use of charters or service guarantees has become widespread, clarifying services, levels of service performance including response times to enquiries, and also identifying the implications for the customer should the service fail to match its promise.

Table 4.1 Approaches to managing expectations

Type	Advantages	Disadvantges
1 Informal agreement	• Easy • Convenient • Informal	• Too vague • Lack of awareness • No agreed review
2 Charter	• Popular and established approach • Halfway stage • Flexible and easily revised • Can stipulate responsibilities- as well as rights	• Insufficient detail • Capable of ambiguity and misunderstanding • Not particularly rigorous
3 Service level agreement	• Clarifies the service which can be expected • Service providers become accountable for the delivery and quality of the service • Customers become aware of the costs of the service and modifications • Measurable standards which help to define service and individual priorities	• Levels and standards need to be realistic • Changes to the level or cost of the service will require renegotiation • Responsibilities of the customer must be made clear • Can be seen as inflexible and devolving authority
4 Core and tailored	• Encourages dialogue and • Enables the service to be tailored to specific needs - more cost-effective? • The shape of things to come?	• Needs excellent negotiating skills • Difficult to reconcile conflicting demands • If resources are reduced the tailored services may be seen as optional

Service level agreements

What are they and why are they important?

> The use of service level agreements has developed within some larger organizations. The SLA takes the charter principles a stage further with increased emphasis on specifying and monitoring performance. It is a key part of the move towards quality and accountability in organizations. The SLA emphasizes the importance of the relationship between the 'internal' customer and the service provided and is a form of contract between two departments or sections within the same organization.

Components of a service level agreement

> ➤ The SLA identifies the provider and customer of the service and specifies the nature of the service(s) provided and the level of service – the timescales, scope and may incorporate limitations.
> ➤ It should clarify the customer responsibilities (if appropriate) and may include details of refunds/compensation if things do not go to plan.
> ➤ Finally, it may also include charges, which incorporate a sliding scale if the service is to be amended.

> The advantage of the SLA is that it clarifies the service which can be expected and therefore should lead to more realism. Service providers also become accountable for the delivery of the service and its quality. Finally, customers become aware of the costs of the service and, in particular, the cost of changing their minds!

> The disadvantages include the fact that levels and standards need to be realistic (some transport organizations have extended their journey times to ensure that they reach their targets). As a service provider, you will also need to negotiate changes to the service and the 'responsibilities' of the customer need to be made clear to avoid confusion.

> However, service level agreements are becoming increasingly common as library services see them as a way of clarifying expectations and responsibilities – on both sides; libraries developing SLAs with their

customers and, in turn, beginning to negotiate SLAs with its own internal suppliers – finance, personnel and IT support.

Management for quality

The European model for quality (Figure 4.1) identifies nine components of quality. These include: quality processes; customer satisfaction; policy and strategy; business results and impact on society. The model also stresses the importance of management in developing a quality service. Aspects which are assessed include: people management; leadership and people (staff) satisfaction. The importance of staff in delivering quality services is echoed by all writers on quality. For example, Chase, writing in the *TQM magazine* in 1993, cites nine reasons for the failure of most quality campaigns. Problems cited include the lack of management commitment, lack of management vision and culture change, lack of staff involvement and above all, complacency.

The role of the manager in developing quality library services

➤ As a manager, seeking to develop and maintain quality, it is important to recognize the changing role of the manager and the need to motivate and enthuse rather than tell. It is also vital to visibly support and promote quality at every opportunity.

➤ Recognize that staff are the vital component in the development of quality. According to Tom Peters, as a manager, you should be recruiting staff with 'people skills' as well as specific or professional expertise.

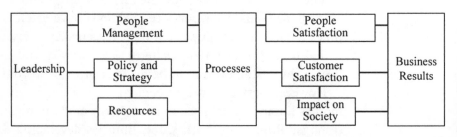

Fig. 4.1 *The European model for quality*

➤ As managers, you also need to think about changing the culture through involving staff at every stage. This reminds us of the importance of communication and involvement which was discussed in Chapter 2. It is also important to motivate staff through providing praise, thanks and positive reinforcement whenever possible.

➤ Training is also crucial to the delivery of quality services. 'Product' or service knowledge is important as well as the more obvious people skills. Providing good induction training and updating staff on a regular basis will help them to be familiar with the full range of services.

➤ Customer satisfaction (internal and external) should be the key measure in all service decisions. It helps to encourage a customer focus if you circulate the results of surveys and customer feedback to staff on a regular basis. Finally, it is necessary to keep the momentum going by sharing and celebrating success and working hard to make staff feel proud of the service.

➤ Above all, as a manager, it is vital to lead by example! The quality-focused manager has zero complacency and encourages feedback from peers, superiors and subordinates to improve their own performance. Complacency is the real enemy of quality and every effort should be made to avoid it in yourself and to ensure that your staff do not succumb either.

Finally, the development of quality library and information services is not an option, it is a necessity. If libraries are to survive in the future, we must demonstrate that our services and our staff are as excellent as they can be. The quality approach can help us to do that.

Summary

It is no longer sufficient today for managers to simply deliver services: the social and political pressures require the delivery of quality services. As a manager you must be able to identify the components of quality of the services for which you have responsibility. This chapter has emphasized the need to develop a customer focus and has given a range of examples of practical ways to develop links with, and manage the expectations of, the most vital element of your job – your customers! Quality is not resource-led – it should be management-led. You have been introduced to some methods and techniques which have been used successfully in the library and information sector. Now think about the strategy you might adopt and the managerial actions you might take, in order to develop your own quality services.

References

Brophy, P., 'BS: a curse or a blessing?', London, *Library Association record*, **96** (6), 1994, 320–1.

Chase, R. L. (ed.), 'Implementing TQM : The best of *The TQM magazine*', London, IFS International, 1993.

Crosby, P., *Quality without tears*, London, McGraw-Hill., 1984.

Ellis, D. and Norton, B., *Implementing BS 5750/ISO 9000 in libraries*, London, Aslib, 1993.

Forrest, A., 'Organisations and people: what difference does an "empowering" or "enabling" culture make'. In *The value of information to the intelligent organisation*, Hatfield, University of Hertfordshire Press, 1994.

Hopson, B. and Scally, M., *12 steps to success through service*, London, Mercury, 1989.

Chapter 5
Managing performance for results

This chapter looks at:

➤ managing performance through setting standards and targets
➤ monitoring performance
➤ personal targets and giving feedback
➤ managing the poor performer
➤ discipline.

Chapter 4 stressed that the need to manage quality is an increasingly important part of every manager's role. One aspect of ensuring quality services is the management of performance and delivery of results at both service and individual level.

There has been considerable interest in the management of performance recently, with the publication of a number of performance measures affecting public and academic libraries. The COSLA performance indicators (for public libraries) and the Effective Library (for academic libraries) both enable organizations to compare the performance of their library service with others in the same sector.

Performance indicators, output measurement and other compulsory assessments mean that every manager is under increased pressure to ensure high performance from his or her service and their staff. Performance measurement should be a vital part of every manager's decision-making as, without good management information, the conclusions drawn about the use or value of a service are likely to be misleading.

Organization's mission
    Department's mission and goals
        Key result areas
            Unit's goals and targets
                Individual's goals and targets
                    Agreed yardsticks of measurement
                        Provision of support and training
                            Regular review and update

Fig. 5.1 *Steps in managing performance*

Chapter 2 looked briefly at some of the components of managing performance, including clarifying the organization's and the department's mission and goals. As a manager, it is helpful to involve staff as much as possible in establishing what you are really there for, as this can encourage involvement and ownership. The next stage is defining local targets and standards, which cascade down as shown in Figure 5.1. These will clearly differ according to the nature of the service and the resources available. The Library Association has recently published *A model statement of standards for public libraries* (1995) which aims to assist local authorities to develop standards and targets appropriate to their local circumstances. The standards cover access, environment and facilities, stock, information services, staff and marketing. The statement also suggests that library authorities should publish an annual statement which evaluates its performance against the standards. The evaluation should be made available to the public **on request**, together with regular surveys of customer satisfaction.

Commercial services, which often have a specialized clientèle, usually have more definite and challenging targets. For example, the targets for a large, publicly funded information unit which serves scientists and works to contract are shown in Figure 5.2.

Literature searches (online, CD-ROM)	15% same day 25% following day 37% within 2–5 working days 23% within 15 working days
Service hours	9.00–5.00 every working day
Interlibrary loans	10% within 10 days 80% within 15 days 10% within 20 days
Book loans	80% within 3 days 20% within 10 days
Enquiries service (Public)	Available 9.00–5.00 (Monday–Friday) 90% answered same day 10% within 10 days
All written enquiries within 10 days of receipt (Citizen's Charter)	
Personal enquiries	90% same day 10% within 10 days
Journal distribution	All circulated within 48 hours of receipt

Fig 5.2 *An example of service targets*

Service targets should be stretching but realistic. Targets which are too 'kind' will not challenge people to work hard, or to question the effectiveness of how things are done. Conversely, if service targets are too ambitious and unrealistic, staff will feel cheated and will never be able to experience the job satisfaction that comes from achievement.

Measuring performance

Many libraries, in making promises and pledges about service quality to their customers, have also introduced ways of monitoring the service provided. This can take many forms and includes monthly monitoring which is governed by a checklist, unobtrusive testing – the mystery-shopper approach – where aspects of the service are put to the test by people pretending to be customers, and finally the fully fledged quality inspection, where the whole service is subject to scrutiny from a panel who may be external to the service itself. All these approaches can be seen as threatening by staff and require careful handling and explanation if they are to be introduced in a positive and helpful way.

Components of a quality inspection

➤ **Who** should carry out the inspection?

Should it comprise senior management, peer review, client unit, customers or 'independent' inspectors, or a combination of these?

➤ **Why?** – what is the purpose?

Is it developmental and partnership? or punitive, identifying 'what has gone wrong?' or is it part of the service level agreement, i.e. to review as part of the open accountability process?

➤ **What** should be measured/inspected?

Management information – statistics, performance indicators, other monitoring information

Customer satisfaction – surveys, exit interviews etc.

Physical environment – tidiness, state of repair/decoration, facilities, amount and type of study space, project rooms etc.

Access, outreach and availability, opening and service hours

Ease of use – guiding, location, self-service facilities etc.

Reference, information and enquiry services; availability and approachability of staff

Lending services – different loan periods to suit different needs

Quality of bookstock and other materials/equipment

Customer care/people skills of **all** staff

Publications and guides

Information for customers or specialist services, e.g. user education in academic libraries etc.

➤**When?**

Should notice be given? If so, how long?

How frequently should inspections take place?

➤**How? What approach should be used?**

Discussions with staff and customers

Checklists and observation

Unobtrusive testing

➤**Follow up**

Draft report – checked for accuracy

Action plan with follow up visit if required.

Performance targets

As mentioned above, many libraries are introducing performance targets and standards as part of their approach to quality. This method has two advantages. It allows the provider to be explicit about the level of service which can be offered, thus helping to manage the customers' expectations. It can also help to demonstrate continuous improvement which assists in promoting the service and is motivating for staff. As discussed in Chapter 4, other ways to clarify expectations include service level agreements and market testing the service to ascertain whether that service can be provided more effectively from elsewhere. With the publication of the KPMG report on contracting out public library services (1995), this is a topical issue at the moment and is likely to be the subject of much debate in the profession.

Performance and the individual

Establishing individual targets

Departmental targets, in their turn, help to define an individual's goals and targets. These can be 'soft', i.e. linked with interpersonal aspects or 'hard' including productivity levels which are required from individual members of staff.

The advantages of establishing individual targets are as follows:

➤ to clearly identify roles, responsibilities and expected levels of performance
➤ to develop and train staff and to identify team and individual training requirements
➤ to be able to respond to change and encourage continuous improvement of personal performance
➤ to promote innovation and broaden skills
➤ to focus on priorities, develop individual and team roles and assist in work planning
➤ to improve job satisfaction and provide opportunities for praise/reward.

For targets to be really effective, they should be both **SMART** and **SMURF**.

S	Specific	S	Specific
M	Measurable	M	Measurable
A	Achievable (or agreed)	U	Urgent
R	Relevant (or realistic)	R	Realistic
T	Timed	F	Future focused.

Monitoring individual targets

As a manager, you need to monitor individual and group targets on a regular basis to check that either you are still 'on target', or to enable you to revise them if they are no longer feasible or appropriate. The monitoring should be much more frequent than the annual appraisal. Every three months seems to be the norm in enlightened organizations.

Giving feedback on performance

Giving regular feedback on performance is an essential part of good management. It is important to be clear about what is expected and about the level of performance actually achieved.

The basis of giving feedback is the 1:1 interview. To be effective, this should:

➤ be private, avoiding interruptions and **always** face to face
➤ review the **whole** job and look at any problems in context
➤ be structured and prepared for; both sides should be clear about what they hope to cover and gain from the discussion
➤ look at the past, present and future – on a regular basis
➤ involve a two-way discussion – the manager should aim for 20% talking, 80% listening!
➤ be action orientated – establishing and agreeing targets and timescales and including a date for the next review.

The results of the discussion should be recorded and copied to both parties.

Giving feedback, especially if it is negative, is not always easy. During the interview, as a manager you should:

➤ be specific and objective
➤ have evidence of problems, e.g. dates, complaints etc.
➤ be clear about what you wish to be changed e.g. a particular aspect of behaviour
➤ ask for a response and use open questions whenever possible
➤ provide an opportunity for genuine discussion
➤ summarize regularly to make sure that there is clarity on both sides
➤ seek agreement and positive outcomes and make clear what will happen if there is **no** agreement
➤ summarize and end positively whenever possible.

It is always important to suspend judgment and separate the person from the problem (if there is one). Also, ensure that performance targets are backed up with good communication, opportunities for individual development and support through training, coaching and the other approaches discussed in Chapter 2. Finally, always review targets regularly to ensure that they are still relevant and ensure that, whenever possible, staff receive praise, thanks and recognition for their achievements.

Managing the 'poor' performer

The other side of managing performance is to tackle problems of 'poor' performance. For many people, this is the worst aspect of their job as a manager and, as a result, there has been a tendency to avoid the issue in many organizations. 'Problem' people take up a lot of time and effort, they create hostility and foster stress and anxiety – in themselves and others. However, if poor performance is not tackled, it can have an adverse effect on the morale and motivation of other staff. It is important to remember that people problems often reflect difficulties or uncertainty on both sides. They can also provide a challenge and an opportunity to improve things for everyone.

According to Peter Honey in his book, *Problem people* (1993), there are four possible approaches:

1. Do nothing
2. Alter your perception
3. Modify the situation
4. Persuade the problem person to change.

Doing nothing may be appropriate if you judge that the problem is very short-term or that the person is about to leave anyway. However, tempting though it is, ignoring problems of poor performance will be unhelpful for colleagues and may jeopardize things if you want to tackle difficulties in the future.

Altering your perception may be helpful if you realize that you are singling out this person for criticism. It may also be appropriate to modify your view if there are mitigating circumstances which are affecting the individual's behaviour. The solution then may be to modify the situation, but to reserve the right to review within a reasonable period of time and amend as the situation demands.

Dealing with 'problem' people

Problem people must always be tackled on an individual basis. Sadly, there are no blueprints. However, John Adair's model of Action Centred Leadership which we looked at in Chapter 2 does provide useful guidance. Thinking of a way forward which balances the needs of task, team and individual is usually a good starting point.

Exercise 5.1

How would you tackle the following problem?

A member of your staff is late more often than not. This person has a difficult journey and you know that their family circumstances are problematic.

However, other staff are now beginning to notice and you wonder whether s/he is taking advantage of you.

If the **task** is to run a library service, the persistent lateness of a member of staff will be problematic, both in terms of opening up the library, but also, possibly with the effect it will have on the other staff (the team). However, if the person concerned is really having difficulties with their travel and other factors, their **individual** needs will also need to be considered.

Using Adair's model, the best way forward (in the short term) might be to allow the **individual** to come in later than usual and to make up the time they owe during their lunch break or by staying later. However, it would be important to alert the person's colleagues to the circumstances **and** to put a time limit on this arrangement to ensure that a review takes place after a reasonable period. If the situation improves, the individual can revert to their original hours. If not, then other solutions such as a permanent move or revised working hours may have to be considered. The important point is, whenever possible, to take into account the different needs and to try to obtain a balance. We cannot promise you that Adair's model will help on every occasion, but it should provide ideas about a way forward in a number of cases.

The situation described above necessitated the use of the 'quiet word' to tackle a problem of poor performance. In most organizations, there are also rules and procedures covering disciplinary issues which can be helpful in determining a way forward.

Disciplinary rules and procedures

Most organizations have written disciplinary procedures, which have usually been negotiated with the unions or staff representatives. Written rules help to set standards of efficient and safe behaviour; they clarify what is expected of staff which helps to ensure that people work in an acceptable way and provide an agreed form of institutional justice and objectivity in dealing with difficult and often emotional situations.

Written procedures will differ between organizations, but they usually cover:

➤ Timekeeping and absence: authorization, certification
➤ Health and Safety issues: smoking, drinking, hazards, cleanliness
➤ Use of 'company' facilities: telephones, equipment, premises, transport
➤ Discrimination: racial or sexual abuse or discrimination, disability
➤ Prohibitions: insubordination, drinking, gambling
➤ Gross misconduct.

Procedures may seem to be a 'sledgehammer to crack a nut', but they do help:

➤ to provide a consistent and fair method of dealing with alleged failure to observe the rules
➤ to encourage action against misconduct or poor performance at an **early** stage
➤ to advocate improvement for poor performers
➤ to apply the discipline code speedily, consistently and fairly across the organization
➤ to ensure that there is a right of appeal against unfair application of the procedures.

Sample disciplinary procedures

In dealing with disciplinary issues, actions should always be taken which are appropriate to the gravity of the alleged misconduct in question. ACAS (1987) recommends that the following stages be followed, although a number of organizations have shortened processes by combining several elements.

➤ Informal disciplinary action. Used for a minor breach of the rules – the 'quiet word'.
➤ Recorded oral warning. Used if misconduct is repeated despite warnings.
➤ Written warning. Used for more serious or persistent misconduct. The warning should clearly state the improvement required and the action that may be taken if there is a repetition or failure to improve.
➤ Final written warning. This is used where failure continues after a written warning or where the failure is serious but not sufficient to justify dismissal.
➤ Dismissal. Used where failure is persistent or misconduct so serious as to justify dismissal.
➤ Alternatives to dismissal such as demotion or financial penalty.

Dealing with disciplinary matters

Except for informal action, procedures should include the following:

➤ a written statement of the allegations, given to the employee with a copy held by you as the manager;
➤ the opportunity for the employee to reply to the allegations at interview (where they may be accompanied by a friend or union representative);
➤ the right for the employee to appeal against a decision;
➤ periods identified after which the disciplinary award is 'spent'; again, these tend to differ between organizations, although it is usual for verbal warnings to last between six months and one year and written warnings to last from one to two years. If a misconduct is so severe that dismissal is considered and then revoked, the final written warning can apply permanently. However, this must be made clear to the employee in writing, together with the fact that any reoccurrence of the misconduct will result in dismissal.

Gross misconduct

These are serious offences which may result in summary dismissal, e.g. theft, fraud, deliberate falsification of records, fighting, assault, deliberate damage, incapacity owing to drugs or alcohol, serious negligence, sexual or racial harassment. Most organizations specify what constitutes gross misconduct within their terms, but external advice should always be taken where the problems are of a serious nature.

Criminal offences outside employment are not automatically a reason for dismissal. It will always depend on the nature of the job, e.g. loss of driving licence could affect someone whose job is as a driver and the seriousness of the offence. *Discipline, grievance and dismissal* (Morris, 1993), provides some useful examples.

Emergency action

In an emergency situation, you as the manager may immediately have to place an employee on precautionary suspension. In these circumstances, this must be on full pay and only after advice from a more senior manager or personal specialist.

If faced with poor performance, unless it is very minor and easily resolved with a quiet word, it is **always** useful to contact your personnel or human resources department for specialist advice. If there is no one fulfilling that role, organizations such as ACAS or the Industrial Society will sometimes provide guidance. Their addresses are included in Appendix 2.

In cases of poor performance, it is vital to ascertain the facts and be very clear about the seriousness of the problem. A number of books such as the ACAS handbook, *Discipline at work* (1987) and *Discipline, grievance and dismissal* (1993), can provide you with invaluable advice. The other major element is to be absolutely fair. Peter Honey's advice to alter your own perception may be important if you recognize that you are picking on a member of staff for specific criticism, while ignoring similar problems in other staff, or indeed yourself.

When you do tackle poor performance, it is important to:

➤ diagnose the problem as thoroughly as you can

➤ discuss the issue **in private** and ask for the individual's ideas for resolving the problem

➤ resolve to tackle team issues if they are part of the cause

➤ agree the change in behaviour that needs to be made and the timescale for review

➤ monitor the situation and use positive reinforcement whenever possible; for example, if someone who is persistently late makes a real effort to turn up on time, acknowledging their efforts can be very helpful in reinforcing the improvement

➤ review the situation as agreed with the individual and take further steps if they are appropriate.

Finally, if we are honest, we have probably all been poor performers at some stage in our lives. The reasons are many and varied, but do stop to consider whether part of the cause of poor performance is the result of the member of staff **not** knowing what was expected of them, a lack of training or confidence or problems with other members of the team. Using incidents of poor performance to reflect and improve the situation for everybody is the sign of a good manager.

Summary

Managers of library and information services have had to respond to the pressures upon them by becoming more accountable and as a result, have to monitor and demonstrate performance achievement at the individual and service level. This chapter should enable you as a manager to assess the criteria for performance measurement and to enable you to judge whether your service is 'on track' or not. Tackling poor performance is often a difficult area, particularly for new managers: this chapter has suggested a range of methods and approaches which you could adopt.

References

ACAS, *Discipline at work: the ACAS advisory handbook*, London, ACAS, 1987.

Honey, P., *Problem people*, London, IPM, 1993.

Industrial Society, *Communications for managers*, London, Industrial Society, 1994.

The Library Association, *A model statement of standards for public libraries*, London, Library Association, 1995.

Moores, R., *Managing for high performance*, London, Industrial Society, 1994.

Morris, S., *Discipline, grievance and dismissal*, London, Industrial Society Press, 1993.

Chapter 6
Managing self

This chapter looks at:

➤ **the importance of managing ourselves**
➤ **time management**
➤ **managing upwards.**

A key component for the successful manager is their ability to manage themselves. This has two elements – the management of our own time and the way we relate to our organizations, together with the way we manage the future, i.e. keep ourselves and our skills up to date. In Chapter 1, we saw the need for newly appointed managers to balance doing, with achieving results through others. This chapter looks at the personal skills which managers need to ensure that the balance is achieved, while Chapter 7 looks at managing the future.

Time management

One of the largest concerns expressed by newly appointed managers is the difficulty of managing their time. Management is very time consuming and increasingly managers in all sectors are suffering from negative stress as a result of conflicting demands. Recent estimates suggest that managers in the UK spend, on average, longer hours at work than their European counterparts and may also take work home in the evenings and at weekends. Effective time management is therefore important for all managers so that the balance between doing and assisting others to do on your behalf is attained.

Exercise 6.1

Make a list of your 'time bandits', i.e. the factors which adversely affect your time management.

If you can, compare your list to those made by a colleague or friend

Time management is very personal, but this exercise is likely to reveal some common factors. It is usual for time bandits to conform to one of the following categories:

➤ interruptions; Minzberg in his work on management skills, suggested that, on average, a manager is interrupted up to 40 times a day!
➤ experiencing difficulties in saying no
➤ reluctance to delegate or no one to whom you can delegate
➤ wanting to be perfect
➤ crises.

The most important time bandit, and the one that most people seem to forget, is not knowing what we want to achieve, i.e. a lack of planning and prioritizing. This is an area where library staff seem to experience more difficulties than in other professions. This may reflect a reluctance to be proactive, i.e. to anticipate and predict demands rather than respond to them when they have happened. Although it is not always easy, identifying priorities does help you to make choices about work which is important and work which could be left or done to a lesser degree. It is clearly essential that plans and priorities are appropriate to the organization and the next section – managing upwards – stresses the need to 'read the runes', to ensure that your ideas are acceptable and feasible.

Doing things right or doing the right things

There are two key points to remember about managing our time more effectively. Firstly that time management is about being effective not just efficient. This means **Doing the right things** rather than just **Doing**

things right and stresses again the importance of determining your priorities. The other major element is the need to target our efforts according to the importance of the job. According to Ken Blanchard, 'A job not worth doing is **not** worth doing well'. Yet for many in library and information work, there is a reluctance to accept the concept of 'good enough' and as a result, we perhaps devote the same amount of energy and effort to every task regardless of its importance.

The principles of managing time more effectively

Time management is a personal matter and it is important that you develop a system that works for you. Being organized does not mean adopting expensive systems or being so organized that you become inflexible. What it does mean is allowing time for the things that matter to you, including those things that are spontaneous. Do not allow time management to make you too rigid to enjoy life. However, there are some principles which might help you to feel more in control.

Defining priorities

Try to determine your priorities and do not attempt to do everything at once. This should include making a daily 'to do' list, preferably the day before. You should then organize the list in accordance with three criteria:

➤ the importance/urgency of the task
➤ the amount of time available
➤ the quality of time available, i.e. your best time and whether you are likely to be interrupted or not.

Good time managers know their own 'best' time, i.e. when they are more alert. Larks prefer the morning, owls are at their best later in the day. You may not always be able to do it, but if you **can** schedule more difficult or complex tasks when you are at your peak, they will feel less daunting.

As a manager, it is vital to do the important as well as the urgent. The challenge for the manager is to work out what is *really* important – not always easy. Working smarter, i.e. doing the right things, is also vital. Figure 6.1 might help you to determine which is which.

High urgency

Delegate Low	**Do first** High
importance **Leave**	importance **Planning**

Low urgency

Fig. 6.1 *Time management grid*

Important and urgent	Do first
Important but less urgent	Start to plan and put in a bring forward system
Urgent but not important	Delegate
Neither urgent or important	Leave unless you really enjoy doing it, but do not spend too much time on it!

The other principles of effective time management include the following:

➤ **Do not procrastinate**. Procrastination is the thief of time and makes quite simple tasks become increasingly daunting. According to Mark Twain, 'If you have to eat a frog don't look at it too long. If you have to eat two frogs – don't eat the smallest one first.'

➤ **Elephant eating** is a good way to avoid procrastination and tackle daunting tasks. Elephant eating involves breaking a large complex task into a series of 'bitesize chunks'. This has two major advantages. Firstly, the task is no longer so daunting, it is now a series of smaller more manageable tasks. Secondly, some of the tasks may be capable of delegation. The use of elephant eating is shown in Figure 6.2.

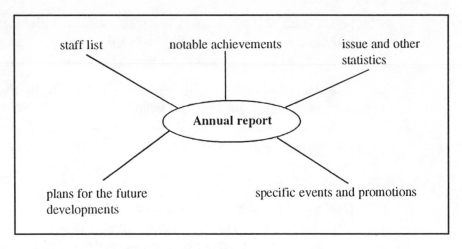

staff list   notable achievements   issue and other statistics

Annual report

plans for the future developments   specific events and promotions

Fig. 6.2 *An example of elephant eating*

Elephant eating also allows you to tackle aspects of the major task in those short blocks of time which seem to be the norm for most library staff. Happy munching!

Becoming assertive: learning to say 'no' or 'not yet'

Developing the skills of assertiveness is an important element in managing our time more effectively. One of the major causes of frustration is people taking on work which is not appropriate or working to deadlines which are unrealistic. However, as a manager, you should learn to be ruthless with time, gracious with people. Learn to say 'no', or 'not yet', in a pleasant but firm way.

The stages in **saying no** are as follows. Assess whether the other person's request is reasonable and ask for information or clarification if you are not sure. You may need to practise saying **NO** and always make the refusal short and direct. Long-winded excuses seem to make the situation worse. Body language is also important. You need to be pleasant, but smiling or being 'nice' is inconsistent and can lead to confusion. Finally, remember you are saying no to the request . . . not the person.

Sometimes, however, it is helpful to negotiate a way forward which is acceptable to both sides. This is called a **workable compromise** and, to be achievable, it needs good listening skills, a willingness to look for common ground and the ability to build on ideas to find a way forward Examples of the workable compromise include:

➤ 'I can't work late tonight; however, I might be able to do it on Thursday if someone can swap.'
➤ 'I will not be able to finish the report by next week. However I should be able to let you have a draft copy by then.'

Dealing with interruptions

Dealing with interruptions is linked to saying no. As a manager, you will want to feel that you operate an open-door policy and are accessible to staff. However, the danger with this is that you will never get a minute's peace and your staff may forget how to make decisions for themselves.

There are a number of 'tricks' to dealing with interruptions:

➤ Be conscious of the cost of your time and encourage others to do the same.
➤ Identify who needs access to you at all times and try to 'manage' the rest.
➤ If you have something important to finish, shut your door if you can, or do deals with your colleagues over answering the telephone or being available to callers.
➤ Develop a system of appointments which help you to be in control.
➤ Go to see staff in their offices or stand up when people come to see you.
➤ Have a clock in a prominent position.
➤ Encourage people to be succinct . . . 'I can spare you one minute'.
➤ Consider answerphones or voicemail to give you some uninterrupted time.
➤ Practise being assertive – learn to say 'no' or, at least, 'not yet'.

Dealing with paperwork

➤ Maintain a tidy desk. Try to keep it clear of other paperwork when you are concentrating on something important.

> Develop collective **bring forward** and other systems which can help you to manage and reduce the amount of duplicate paperwork.
> Try to weed paperwork on a regular basis – one of the best time-management tools is a large black bin bag!
> Try to handle paper only once: **action it: file it: pass it on: bin it.**

Other time management tips

> Allocate time for tasks (and add 20%).
> Note key dates – end of financial year, start of academic year, annual report due. This helps you to anticipate delays and to plan and prioritize your work and help others to plan theirs.
> Try to target some 'private' time when you can think and plan your work. Five minutes' planning every day is supposed to save you at least one hour of actually doing!
> Use 'committed' time, e.g. travel time profitably. Read, make notes or just switch off. Probably the best thing to ask yourself on a regular basis is 'What is the best use of my time **now**?'
> Group similar tasks together and resolve to make, for example, five telephone calls in a given time.
> Do the things that everyone else needs to do . . . at a time when they are not doing them! This applies to non-work activities such as shopping as well as work tasks.
> Recognize your own quality time and use it well.

Time management tips that relate specifically to library problems include:

> identifying the most popular enquiries (the Frequently Asked Questions) and producing helpsheets or guides which can be given to users as a first resort;
> monitoring the use of the library and allocate staff to counters and enquiry desks accordingly; linked with this, libraries are beginning to develop data banks of standard questions to help to provide a consistent response and to save staff time; increasingly, these will be made available to customers over networks;

➤ developing an appointments system for 'professional' support and expertise; this is increasingly used in academic libraries to help balance staff resources against potential demand;

➤ encouraging self-help for users and customers; for example, develop information skills' sessions which help users to feel more confident and run 'drop in' workshops on specific sources such as CD-ROM;

➤ good staff training and sharing expertise can help to spread the workload;

➤ effective delegation as discussed in Chapter 2 also helps to ensure that work is carried out at the appropriate level;

➤ finally, carrying out a cost/benefit analysis on routine tasks can help to determine whether they **are** being carried out at the right level or possibly, whether they should be done at all!

Managing upwards

The second aspect of managing ourselves is **managing upwards**. Increasingly, it is not just **what** you know that matters in work, it is how and to whom you show it. For example, at a recent meeting between representatives of The Library Association and college principals (Clayton, 1996), senior college managers suggested that their librarians were not always flexible enough and not receptive to new ideas. In addition, they did not seem to 'market' themselves or their services effectively within the college. The emphasis seemed to be on indicating problems rather than proposing solutions and they were accused of lacking political 'awareness'.

Managing upwards involves:

➤ understanding corporate issues, anticipating trends and using strategic management to link and promote the library service to the needs of the organization;

➤ using influencing skills to anticipate and contribute to change;

➤ raising the profile of the service through developing presentation skills and knowing how to make a case;

➤ using negotiating and influencing skills – with different groups such as customers, suppliers, peers and senior managers;

➤ improving the 'image' of the library or information manager;
➤ networking and being cooperative with staff from other disciplines. Tom Peters defines this as the 'corporation as Rolodex' (Peters, 1994).

As well as managing the staff and the service, it is important that managers in all types of library and information units learn to understand and 'manage' the organizations in which they work. Political skills can be seen as mercenary in the library world. However, it is important to remember that all organizations have a political dimension, and this is likely to become more significant as resources diminish.

Political skill includes understanding strategic and corporate issues. The effective library or information manager keeps their ear to the ground and reads widely including corporate information such as development and business plans as well as reading more broadly within the sector. There appears to be a reluctance on the part of some librarians to read the sector's publications on a regular basis. The excuse given is usually a lack of time which brings us back to the importance of effective time management as discussed above. Keeping up to date can help us to anticipate trends and understand why things are happening. It can also help to identify approaches to tackling problems by learning from what others are doing.

Influencing skills

In managing upwards, it is also important to develop good influencing and negotiating skills. Influencing skills are important in ensuring that the service is remembered when resources are being allocated and are also about doing yourself and your staff justice. Influencing skills involve trying to ascertain who will be involved in making a key decision. This is important for two reasons. Firstly, you are identifying any elements of bias which may help or hinder your case. Secondly, you are also looking for 'hooks' on which you might hang arguments or justification. For example, one inner city library authority was able to gain additional resources for their community libraries by linking educational attainment to reading ability and therefore, library use. Similarly, a university library was able to argue for investment in a networked CD-ROM service because a senior manager thought CD-ROM was 'sexy'!

In order to influence decisions, it is important to do your homework as thoroughly as possible. Collect facts and figures which will support your case and will counteract arguments from the other side. It is helpful to think about who could support you by arguing on your side and who may weaken your case if they are seen to support you. It is also important to think about the sort of arguments which make an impact in **your** organization. This will differ between organizations and over time, but it is useful to consider issues which are of current concern in most organizations such as quality, cost effectiveness, income generation or increased custom.

It can sometimes help to find out what they do elsewhere, especially if it is an organization with kudos. It may also be worth mentioning competitors who will benefit if you are **not** able to implement your plans. However, be careful with this one – mention of competitors may antagonize rather than impress the decision makers.

If you are asked to make a presentation as part of your argument, consider which is the most appropriate form. In some organizations, all presentations will be formal. In others, the informal presentation is the norm. It is increasingly important to think about graphics – diagrams or practical examples – as anything which helps to the audience to understand what you are proposing is useful.

Presentation skills

These are increasingly beneficial at all levels. They help to do yourself and your service justice and ensure that any case for support is as professional as it can be. However, very few people are good natural presenters. The three stages to making a good presentation are **preparation**, **persuasion** and **practice**.

Preparation is vital. It helps you to feel more secure and assists in calming your nerves. As well as finding out about your audience and researching your subject, preparation means finding out about the venue and whether you need any equipment for your presentation. It also means sounding out your own ideas and, if necessary, lobbying those likely to be involved in making the decision.

It is also important to marshal your arguments and, if you have not presented in public before, try to rehearse your presentation, preferably in front of a supportive but critical audience. This helps you to feel more confident and allows you to check timings.

Do remember that **resources (or other forms of support) = relevance plus results.** Any arguments you use must therefore be couched in terms which make sense to your audience, not to you! Similarly, have **all** your facts to hand, keep your presentation clear and concise and look as if **you** believe in what you are saying. Use active listening and observe people's body language to gauge their reaction and always try to anticipate questions and objections. This is where practice can also be useful. Finally, it is important to **present solutions not problems.** As we have seen, a common criticism of library and information managers is that they emphasize the problems, without suggesting strategies which could help.

In aiming to influence, you must not expect all your ideas to be welcomed and it is important to be prepared to negotiate an acceptable way forward which enables both sides to gain an advantage and maintain a good relationship.

Negotiating skills are increasing important to all library and information managers, reflecting the need to work well with different groups such as customers, suppliers, peers and senior managers. Figure 6.3 illustrates the different situations in negotiation.

For negotiation to be successful, there must be a genuine desire on both sides, to move forward. The different positions which can be adopted by parties are discussed below.

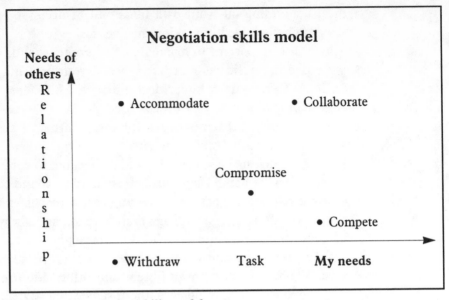

Fig. 6.3 *Negotiation skills model*

Withdrawal

This avoids conflict and may be the result of a lack of confidence in or support from others in the past. However, it does not do the service justice and can be viewed as 'sour grapes' by those who wish to move forward.

Accommodation

This may be the result of the perception of power in the other party or fear of reprisals. It can, however, create resentment and may mean that what **you** have agreed is not upheld by your colleagues. It can, however, be useful in gaining advantage in the future.

Compromise

This can be a quick solution and satisfying to both sides. It also demonstrates a willingness to move forward, but again can lead colleagues to feel that they have been 'let down'.

Competition

This may be the result of fear of being 'done' or your principles being threatened. It can also create a backlash or subversion.

Collaboration

Finally, collaboration is the most effective strategy, as it is aimed at agreeing mutual goals and creating a win/win climate. This does mean a collective and creative approach, which involves sharing information and generating commitment and trust on both sides. However, it encourages cooperation in the future and often the solution obtained is more effective because of the thought and discussion which has gone into it.

Good negotiators need many of the skills that have been discussed in previous chapters. They need to be able to build rapport and create an atmosphere of trust and responsiveness as quickly as possible. They should also be observant and receptive to the other person's way of speaking using excellent listening skills, empathizing with the other person's point of view and suspending judgment or criticism. They need to be clear in their own communication, avoiding ambiguity and, therefore, confusion. This also means using consistent body language to emphasize points they wish to make. Finally, the best negotiators signal their intentions by saying 'Perhaps I could ask for clarification here?' or 'Could I please make a suggestion here?'. This is part of being clear and consistent and prepares the other party for what you are going to say. Following any negotiation, whatever the outcome, make sure you clarify what has been agreed and confirm the decision in writing as soon as possible. Finally, also make sure that you deliver your part of the bargain!

Raising your profile

The final element in managing upwards is to know how to raise the profile of yourself and the service. Good presentation skills and knowing how to make a case are part of this process, but you should also be conscious of the 'image' of the library or information manager and do what you can to challenge and improve this.

According to Harvey Coleman (quoted in Willis, 1993), the way we are judged is a combination of three elements – the work itself, our image within the organization and our 'visibility', i.e. the extent to which people know about our work.

Exercise 6.2

Spend a few minutes thinking about

➤ the way you do your job
➤ your image within the organization
➤ your 'visibility' or the extent to which your work is known.

Which of these seems to be the most important in your organization?

Harvey Coleman's model is illustrated in Fig. 6.4. Note the particular emphasis on visibility. This is important to you as a manager, because it suggests that even if your work is excellent, it will make little difference unless you also promote yourself and have regard to the image you present.

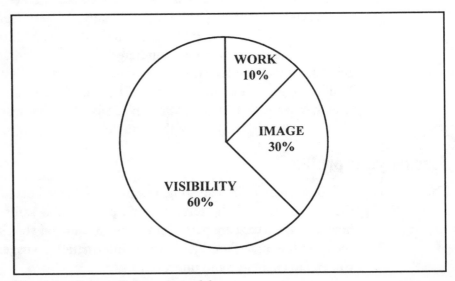

Fig. 6.4 *Harvey Coleman's model*

Improving our visibility is, however, risky. Some people may not like us for it, but they may be the ones who feel threatened themselves. It is important to remember that, as a manager, you cannot and should not expect to be liked all the time. The role of the manager means that, if you are doing your job properly, you will inevitably come into conflict with people occasionally. This does not mean that you should 'court' trouble, rather that you should not be surprised if you upset someone along the way.

Improving your visibility

Improving your visibility involves a number of elements. It is important to keep yourself well informed and take an interest in corporate issues and trends. This will help to understand why changes are happening and to anticipate 'challenges' for the future

Increasing your visibility links with using a marketing approach in developing the service. Promotional activities such as newsletters; open days and other events help to raise the profile of the service and yourself. Other aspects may be less obvious such as attending social events, volunteering for work which helps you to understand more about the organization or getting involved in projects which provide an opportunity to work with different groups of staff. Some of these activities also provide useful opportunities to improve your skills and experience. Whatever approach you use to raise your profile, the most important point is to ensure that everything you do is responsive to the changing needs of the organization. You can deliver the best profile-raising event in the world, but if it is ignorant of the strategic issues and corporate concerns, in the long run, it will do more harm than good.

Summary

We have defined management as achieving results through others. It is equally important for the managers themselves to have or to develop a range of skills to enable them to operate effectively at a personal level. This chapter has covered the principal skills: you should now be aware of the importance of effective time management and a range of practical suggestions have been given to enable you to manage your own time. You should also understand that a key part of management is managing upwards, which can manifest itself as negotiating and influencing, presentation and profile raising. A range of approaches have been suggested which you could use as a guide for developing your own skills.

References

Clayton, C., 'Lack of status due to image problem', London, *Library Association record*, **98** (1), 1996, 20

Covey, S., *Seven habits of highly effective people*, Berkeley, California, Simon and Schuster, 1992.

Hopson, B. and Scally, M., *12 steps to success through service*, London, Mercury, 1989.

Peters, T., *The Tom Peters seminar*, London, Macmillan, 1994.

Willis, L., *Springboard*, London, Hawthorn Press, 1990.

Chapter 7
Managing the future

This chapter looks at:

➤ employability and employment
➤ personal and professional development
➤ management skills for the millennium.

Influencing change

Throughout this book, we have looked at the various skills needed by successful managers. These have included the skills needed to manage people, as individuals and as teams. It has also covered the need to manage ourselves – our own time and the way we manage upwards. However, there is another skill which has become increasingly significant over the last decade and that is the need to manage the future. This involves understanding the strategic and corporate issues which were discussed in Chapter 6 as well as being able to anticipate and take account of trends in developing the service. The ability to influence change is also vital and links with the skill of managing upwards.

According to Tom Peters, 'The only job security is to be more talented tomorrow than you are today'. Writers such as Peters and William Bridges consider the pace of change to be so rapid that only managers who are able to reinvent themselves will thrive in the future. Similarly, supporting and motivating our staff through incessant change will demand different skills from managing during a more stable time.

Employability rather than employment

The future is becoming even more uncertain with an emphasis on employability rather than employment (Peters, 1994). Library and information staff need to be able to adapt to changing circumstances and be prepared to take on different and possibly more challenging tasks. It is also important to recognize that rapid change creates uncertainty and anxiety. Change threatens our competence and confidence; it can have an adverse effect on the relationships we develop with colleagues and, if we are honest, can also affect our status and self-esteem.

Supporting staff through rapid change

Managing rapid change means anticipating change as much as possible and planning ahead as much as you can. As a manager, you should be aware of the 'billiard ball' effect, i.e. change bringing about unexpected consequences, and you should also try to understand the impact of too much change – your staff can become overwhelmed and overloaded. The effective manager tries to negotiates with their own manager(s) to try to ensure that any promises made are as realistic as possible.

Support for staff is particularly important during rapid and major change. If people feel threatened, it will affect the quality of their work and their energies will be diverted. Managing change means recognizing that every change involves an ending and, as an effective manager, acknowledging the links with the past rather than trying to deny or ridicule them. Many staff feel that a change in priorities for whatever reason means that their previous work was a waste of time. It is essential to challenge this assumption, for it leads to staff feeling undervalued and lowers morale.

William Bridges in *Managing transitions* (1991) calls a period of rapid change the 'neutral zone' because everything – systems, relationships and skills – are unreliable and uncertain. The neutral zone is clearly a time of high anxiety, but it can also provide an opportunity to challenge the *status quo* and to identify creative and innovative ways to tackling problems. Bridges suggests that, as managers, we may need to create temporary systems to provide some stability and we should also encourage short-term projects which provide a chance for staff to experience achievement. The appointment of 'change champions', people with influence can also help to take staff with them.

Rapid change will certainly necessitate training for staff in any new skills they will need. As a manager, you too will need to be trained and supported. This is a particularly anxious time for those who have to implement changes as they are likely to be the object of any blame. As a manager, it is important **not** to take criticism personally, as the comments are aimed at your role rather than you. Having said that, the skills we discussed in Chapter 2, active listening, encouraging staff (and customers) to express concerns and misunderstandings and improving communication – explaining what is happening and clarifying the reasons for the change – are all crucial. It is also useful at this stage to sell problems rather than solutions, i.e. encourage staff to challenge the way things are done at the moment. According to Bridges, the 'neutral zone' is the best time to foster risk and creativity.

Another aspect which helps in implementing change is to promote a vision of the future which introduces staff to the new beginning. Howard Gardner in his new book, *Leading minds: an anatomy of leadership* (1995), proposes that 'telling a story', i.e. talking in pictures, is one of the six 'constants' of recognized leaders. Promoting the new beginning through purpose, pictures and plans is an important element in encouraging staff (and customers) to adapt to the new circumstances. Equally important, however, is ensuring the reality matches the rhetoric i.e. that management's actions are consistent with their words. Another useful approach is to ensure and celebrate early success. This can be achieved by the use of short, sharp projects as outlined above, especially those which have a good chance of success. Providing opportunities for staff to experience success can do wonders for flagging motivation and morale.

Management for the millennium

The workplace of the future is going to need different skills again. In *The fifth discipline*, Peter Senge's book about how companies can become 'learning organizations' (1990), the author stresses that the organizations that excel in the future, will be those that discover how to tap their staff's commitment and capacity to learn. Warren Bennis and others suggest that the manager of the future will need to be a facilitator and coach rather than just lead their staff. This new approach is called **transformational management,** and advocates of it such as Tom Peters and Sir John Harvey Jones suggest that it demands even greater skill on the part of the manager. The role of the manager in these circumstances is to lead from behind through empowering and encouraging staff rather than being authoritative. As the manager, you will still need to clarify direction and establish goals, but transformational management emphasizes the contribution of each individual to the workplace.

Training and development

Transformational management also recognizes that training and support for staff is vital and advocates continuous development through innovative approaches such as in-company staff development centres or Ford's Employee Development Assistance Programme (EDAP) which enables staff to carry out training or study which is **not** job related. The theory behind this scheme is that if people are learning something relevant to them, they will be more motivated and feel that their job provides more satisfaction. The EDAP scheme has been modified and adopted by a number of other organizations including the Rover Group and Oxford Brookes University. A by-product of the scheme is that it attracts groups of staff such as cleaners and porters who have not always benefited from the more traditional approach to staff development.

Managers who are aiming to become transformational managers will need to respect and trust their staff and involve them in decision-making. Andrew Forrest in a paper to the UK library technology fair Libtech 93 (Forrest, 1994) identifies different ways to encourage involvement and feedback from staff including suggestions schemes, quality circles and management by walking about. Equally important is an approach to communication which covers the broader issues as well as the detail so that staff can see their work in context. Teamwork is also seen as vital to this new environment and Forrest identifies examples of organizations such as Body Shop where staff are involved in selecting their colleagues. In these circumstances, the manager's role becomes that of cheerleader, mentor and coach and he or she should do all they can to create a culture of creativity which encourages innovation and risk and does not penalize mistakes.

The manager of the new millennium

The importance of personal and professional development

If Tom Peters is correct and the only job security is to be more talented tomorrow than we are today, as managers, there is a need to take seriously our own personal and professional development. It is not just organizations who need to think about continuous improvement!

Personal and professional development is important for every library and information manager, to demonstrate their commitment to the job by developing their own skills on a regular basis. It also gives a powerful message to their staff that we are all capable of improving our own skill and competence. As Barry Hopson and Mike Scally say in their book, *12 steps to success through service* (1989), 'You don't have to be ill to get better!'

According to Stephen Covey in *The seven habits of highly effective people* (1992), sharpening the saw, i.e. looking to improve our skills and competence, is very important for the reasons outlined above. He also suggests that we should aim to achieve the following:

- ➤ be proactive
- ➤ begin with an end in mind
- ➤ put first things first
- ➤ think win/win
- ➤ seek first to understand, then be understood
- ➤ synergize.

Taking responsibility

Being proactive is crucial to our personal and professional development. Although other people can support (or hinder) you in your endeavours, the ultimate responsibility will always lie with you. Part of being proactive is to recognize that career opportunities do not just happen.

Successful managers stress that they have usually created their own opportunities.

Personal and professional development involves a number of stages and, again incorporating Covey's 'habits', it is important to begin with an end in mind. Career goals are vital to personal and professional development, even if they are rather sketchy at first. Goals provide a sense of direction and also help us to make choices and identify priorities. However, career goals should never be written in concrete. As with any goal, they should be reviewed on a regular basis to see if they are still current or attainable.

Writers on self-development such as Tom Peters and Sir John Harvey Jones stress that it is important to know your own strengths and weaknesses. Carrying out a regular audit of your strengths, weaknesses and what you want out of life helps you to see if you are still on target to attain your goals. The Library Association's CPD Framework, mentioned in Chapter 2 provides a useful reminder of the stages and suggests practical approaches to developing skills and competence. If it is important to your future, resolve to work on your weaknesses or find ways to compensate for them, e.g. by cooperating with other staff with different skills to your own.

There are a variety of ways to improve your skills and confidence. The most obvious is some sort of training course or longer course leading to a qualification. The current focus on 'lifelong learning' is creating new opportunities in further and higher education. There are courses in management for library and information staff, ranging from diploma to MBA level, there are also top-up qualifications specializing in information technology, strategic management and many other aspects. Recent initiatives in HE include distance learning and part-time courses, some of which allow credit for previous experience. Outside library and information work, there is a miscellany of courses focusing on personal management, IT, financial and resource management. Increasingly, they are being taught in a flexible way with various modes of attendance. Finally, the Information and Library Lead Body has recently published the criteria for NVQs in the field. It is now possible to gain a (degree-level) award based solely on work experience and plans are in train for a masters' level qualification. Other approaches to personal and professional development include voluntary and professional activities which can be useful in filling 'gaps' in your skills. They can also help to develop team-work and leadership skills and provide an understanding of financial and commercial issues.

Other possibilities include looking for opportunities to improve your experience and confidence within your organization. Secondments, exchanges and contributing to working parties or project groups can help you to develop new skills and also provide useful contacts. As we saw in Chapter 6, it is also important to keep yourself up to date, by reading widely and by considering strategic as well as professional issues. Finally, do try to anticipate developments and trends within your sector. This can be done by keeping up to date, by learning to 'read the runes', i.e. watching for signs and signals in your organization and by learning from what is happening elsewhere. You may not always be correct in your predictions, but you and your service will usually have a head start on many of your colleagues as a result.

One of the major tensions with thinking about personal and professional development is making sufficient time. Many library staff are having to reduce their professional and other commitments as the pressure of work increases. This is where Covey's third 'habit' is important – learning to put first things first. Making time for your own development and that of your staff should be a priority for every manager. This will necessitate the use of assertiveness skills, influencing skills and sometimes thinking the unthinkable, i.e. doing things differently or not at all. In library and information work, there sometimes seems to be a reluctance to learn from the experience of other sectors or professions – the 'not invented here' syndrome. Tomorrow's manager will not have time to reinvent the wheel and will need to look at how the changes he or she is facing have been tackled elsewhere. Sometimes inspiration can come from an unlikely source. For example, a recent Channel 4 television series on the development of the Boeing 777 passenger aircraft was principally about innovative ways of managing change, rather than aeronautics.

Conclusion

You, as a manager approaching the new millennium, will need to work to a very demanding agenda:

➤ Meeting these challenges head on, becoming adaptable and flexible and feeling confident in your own abilities and those of your staff.

➤ Transferring and adapting ideas, strategies, solutions and techniques from other library and information sectors; more importantly, learning from experience in other areas which have undergone major change, e.g. privatized industries, sectors facing new competition and business mergers (and de-mergers) etc.

➤ Learning to work smarter rather than harder – achieving maximum results from optimum effort by managing our time, being creative and learning from elsewhere.

➤ Learning to live with ambiguity and providing solutions rather than problems. 'If we can keep our heads, while all around are losing theirs . . .'.

➤ Adopting a more critical and questioning role, challenging the *status quo* . . . 'why do we do this? . . . how could we do it better/cheaper? . . . what if we . . . ?'.

➤ Developing a more 'dynamic' approach to working within our organizations, by being proactive, taking the initiative and not always waiting to be asked.

➤ Thinking win/win, i.e. learning to negotiate with colleagues who may be from different disciplines and with varied skills and experience.

➤ Marketing and promoting your services at every opportunity and in a way which makes sense to your customers.

➤ Learning to communicate – seeking first to understand, then be understood.

➤ Listening to your customers – they are your most powerful advocate.

➤ Demonstrating our performance (and value) and expressing success in terms your customers and managers can readily understand and relate to.

➤ Improving your employability in the future; we must take responsibility for ourselves and our development, finding support for ourselves and offering support to others.

Perhaps we should let Sir John Harvey Jones have the last word. The challenge for the manager is to 'Create, lead, inspire and motivate teams of people who, by their creativity . . . dedication and relevance to the needs of tomorrow will ensure that their business gets to the front and stays there.' We hope this book will help you with the challenges that lie ahead.

References

Bridges, W., *Managing transitions*, London, McGraw-Hill, 1991.

Covey, S., *Seven habits of highly effective people*, Berkeley, California, Simon and Schuster, 1992.

Harvey-Jones, Sir J., *All together now*, London, William Heinemann, 1991.

Peters, T., *The Tom Peters seminar*, London, Macmillan, 1994.

Appendix 1: Further reading

Chapter 1 The challenge of management

Belasco, J. A., *Teaching the elephant to dance*, London, Century Business, 1990.
   An interesting and quirky book about managing change
Nicholson, J., *How do you manage?*, London, BBC Books, 1992.
   Good introduction to management approaches including motivation and teamwork. Contains a number of practical exercises and quizzes.
Semler, R., *Maverick*, London, Arrow, 1994.
   Another unusual look at management.

Chapter 2 Managing people

Barsoux, J., *Funny business*, London, Cassell, 1993.
   The use of humour in management – great fun and excellent cartoons!
Harvey-Jones, Sir J., *Making it happen: reflections on leadership*, London, Heinemann, 1988.
   Charismatic style and a good storyteller.
Lawes, A. (ed.), *Management skills for the information manager*, London, Ashgate, 1993.
   Useful introduction to many facets of management. Aimed at information specialists.
Levy, P., *Interpersonal skills*, London, Library Association Publishing, 1993.
O' Riley, P., *The skills development handbook for busy managers*, London, McGraw-Hill, 1993.
   Useful overview of management skills – very practical and readable.

Chapter 3 Managing effective teams

Hardingham, A. and Royal, J., *Pulling together: teamwork in practice*, London, Institute of Personnel and Development, 1994.

Good introduction to the essential aspects.

Leigh, A. and Maynard, M., *Leading your team*, London, Nicholas Brealey, 1995.

Useful and interesting.

Morris, S. *et al.*, *How to lead a winning team*, London, Institute of Management, 1995.

Good introduction to the essential elements.

Chapter 4 Delivering quality library services

Atkinson, P. E., *Creating culture change: the key to successful total quality management*, London, IFS Publications, 1990.

Bell, D, McBride, P and Wilson, G., *Managing quality*, London, Institute of Management, 1994.

Chase, R L. (ed.), *Implementing TQM: The best of* The TQM Magazine, London, IFS International, 1993.

Hopson, B. and Scally, M., *12 steps to success through service*, London, Mercury, 1989.

Excellent overview of what excellence is and why it matters. Also covers customer surveys, standard setting and dealing with complaints.

Martin, D., *Total quality management*, London, LITC (Library and Information Briefings 45), 1993.

Succinct introduction to quality concepts.

Murphy, J. A., *Service quality in practice: a handbook for practitioners*, London, Gill and Macmillan, 1993.

Relates quality to public sector. Useful and interesting.

Chapter 5 Managing performance for results

Moores, R., *Managing for high performance*, London, Industrial Society, 1994.

Readable and short book about managing performance.

Morris, S., *Sensitive issues in the workplace: a practical handbook*, London, Industrial Society, 1993.

Useful guidance about difficult and sensitive areas.

Stewart, V. and Stewart, A., *Managing the poor performer*, London, Gower, 1982.

Chapter 6 Managing self

Arroba, T. and James, K., *Pressure at work*, 2nd edn, London, McGraw-Hill, 1992.

Useful introduction into managing stress through being assertive.

Bliss, E., *Getting things done: the ABC's of time management*, revised edition, London, Macmillan, 1991.

Practical ideas for being better organized.

Buzan, T., *Radiant thinking*, London, BBC Books, 1993.

The mind map book. Useful and inspirational.

Dale, M., *Developing management skills*, London, Kogan Page, 1993.

Gillen, T., *Positive influencing skills*, London, IPD, 1995.

Peters, T., *The Tom Peters seminar*, London, Macmillan, 1994.

Sampson, E., *The image factor*, London, Kogan Page, 1994.

Chapter 7 Managing the future

Bolles, R., *What color is your parachute?*, 11th edn, Berkeley, California, Ten Speed Press, 1994.

Classic American career development text.

Bridges, W., *Jobshift*, London, Allen and Unwin, 1995.

Looks to the future and the changing employment patterns. Challenging and interesting.

Carnall, C, A., *Managing change in organizations*, London, Prentice-Hall, 1990.

Useful book on the impact of change on ourselves and the organization.

Drucker, P., *Managing for the future*, London, Butterworth Heinemann, 1992.

Thought-provoking and interesting.

Forrest, A., *Fifty ways to personal development*, London, Industrial Society, 1995.

Useful summary of approaches to personal development. Some unusual ideas.

Hardington, A., *Making change work for you*, London, Sheldon, 1992.

Harvey-Jones, Sir J., *All together now*, London, Heinemann, 1994.

The manager as maestro – thought provoking.

Reeves, T., *Managing effectively. Developing yourself through experience*, London, Butterworth Heinemann, 1994.
Ways to learn from experience and useful skills.

Weaver-Mayers, R., 'If you can't go . . . grow!', papers presented at the ALA Annual Conference, New Orleans, 1993, *Library administration and management*, **9** (1), 1994, 12–26.
Practical ways to cope with a career plateau.

White, J., *Frogs or chameleons*, London, Library Association, 1993.
A report commissioned by the Library Association into the skills needed by public library staff in the future.

Appendix 2 Some useful organizations

Advisory Conciliation and Arbitration Service (ACAS)

Clifton House
83–117 Euston Road
London NW1 2RB
☎0171 396 5100
Fax: 0171 396 5159

A good source of advice and information. Has a number of local offices
and publishes useful booklets.

Industrial Society

48 Bryanston Square
London W1H 7LN
☎ 0171 262 2401
Fax: 0171 706 1096

Has regional offices and a number of specialist sections. Runs a number
of management courses, publishes useful and straightforward books and
offers an advisory service on management topics to members.

The Library Association

7 Ridgmount Street
London W1E 7AE
☎ 0171 636 7543
Fax: 0171 436 7218
    0171 636 3627 (LA Publishing)
    e-mail: info@la-hq.org.uk
        lapublishing@la-hq.org.uk

Information and advice for members and employers. Successful Continuing Development programme which covers many of the topics covered in this book.

Library Association Publishing publishes a range of practical and theoretical professional development materials for managers in the LIS field. For further details contact their sales and marketing department on the numbers above.

TFPL

17–18 Britton Street
London EC1M 5NQ
☎ 0171 251 5522
Fax: 0171 251 8318
e-mail: 100067.1560@compuserve.com
Web site: www.tfpl.com

Commercial organization in the information field, which offers training courses and conferences on current topics.

Index